Teacher-Made Tests

Teacher-Made Tests

by JOHN A. GREEN

COLLEGE OF EDUCATION, UNIVERSITY OF IDAHO

HARPER & ROW, PUBLISHERS

NEW YORK, EVANSTON,

AND LONDON

LIBRARY OF CONGRESS CATALOG CARD NUMBER: 63–11297

Contents

v

Preface

Teachers, from elementary school to university, often approach final-exam periods reluctantly, as if they have little confidence in the examination procedure. Since good teaching is difficult without an evaluation to identify areas of student strengths and weaknesses, this reluctance must stem either from teachers' misunderstanding of the intimate tie between instruction and evaluation, or from a lack of confidence in their ability to construct valid, reliable measurement instruments. With the former assumption in mind, the stress throughout the book has been upon the intimate relationship between instructional objectives and evaluation objectives.

Every effort has been made to include the most important suggestions for insuring correlated instruction and measurement. As each of the different types of teacher-made tests is discussed, its strengths and weaknesses are noted, suggestions for improving the use of evaluating instruments are given, and specific rules and practical examples are presented to aid the teacher in constructing his own test.

Throughout the book the stress is placed on practical applications of testing rather than on an abstract measurement theory, although in some instances theoretical discussion has been included as the prerequisite to practical considerations.

In addition to the chapters dealing specifically with the construction and use of the various test forms, two chapters give consideration to related topics. Chapter 8 is devoted to scoring and grading examinations and to assigning course marks. Chapter 9 includes an elementary discussion of the statistics used in summarizing and interpreting test data.

The book should be useful as a text in test-construction classes and as a supplementary text in methods and measurement courses. In addition, it is hoped that experienced teachers can use the book to improve their testing procedures and thus improve the quality of their instruction. If this purpose is achieved, the author will feel that his efforts in writing the book were amply justified.

I wish to express my sincere gratitude to numerous graduate students in my measurement classes whose constructive criticism contributed to this book, to my colleagues at the University who encouraged me to complete the project, and to my wife who acted as both critic and typist for the final manuscript.

J. A. G.

Teacher-Made Tests

CHAPTER 1 *Instruments and criteria of measurement*

INTRODUCTION

High-quality teaching is a professional task which takes years of preparation, careful planning, and skillful execution; and the learning which results from such teaching cannot be guessed at or judged intuitively. In fact successful teaching demands accurate, comprehensive assessment of learning at the beginning of the school year to establish the level at which instruction should begin; during the year to show the rate and extent of progress; and at the end of the year to show the ultimate achievement of each pupil. Obviously, then, measurement objectives must coincide with instructional objectives.

Yet it is not unusual to find a teacher who has had no specific training in measurement and evaluation and who has evolved his testing procedures through trial and error. Such a teacher often designs tests which measure objectives other than those which have been emphasized in his classroom. Because his examinations emphasize trivial points which had been either neglected in class or given only cursory consideration, he has little notion of the effectiveness of

1

his instructional objectives. For this teacher tests may become a series of puzzles designed to fool the student instead of instruments for measuring the relative attainment of classroom objectives.

The point which will be stressed repeatedly throughout this chapter is that measurement objectives of teacher-made tests should be the same as the instructional objectives, if the tests are to have worthwhile instructional functions other than the assignment of marks to pupils.

TEST FUNCTIONS

When classified according to their functions, tests fall into three categories: (1) instructional tests, (2) mastery tests, and (3) measurement tests. Each of these tests has a different difficulty level, and each employs different criteria of measurement.

The first type, the *instructional test,* has instruction as its major purpose. It is a relatively easy test which is designed to give the pupil some understanding of his strengths and weaknesses and at the same time emphasize and reinforce those important points which he is to learn and remember. Such a test is often graded by the pupils, or it is graded by the teacher and handed back to the pupils for class discussion. This discussion permits maximum learning to result from the test experience: it helps the pupils to clear up misunderstandings and recall the facts which they had forgotten while writing the test. Because the primary purpose of this type of test is instructional, the test scores are not generally weighed heavily as a factor in the class grade.

In many subject-matter areas it is necessary that the pupil master certain basic competencies before proceeding to the next level of learning. The second type of test, the *mastery test,* is used by the teacher to determine when the pupils have achieved sufficient competence to proceed to more difficult learning tasks. It is essential, for example, that all pupils master the multiplication tables before they proceed to more complex multiplication and division problems. The mastery test covers the essential learnings, yet it is not difficult because all the pupils will be expected to answer correctly 90 percent or more of the items. For this type of test the pupils should be informed ahead of time of the exact areas to be covered, and they should thus be able to anticipate most of the questions. In this way their study can be directed toward the specific learnings to be mastered.

The mastery test is particularly useful in such basic skill areas as grammar and mathematics, since it permits the teacher to pace instruction according to the learning rate of the majority of the pupils. Without such testing, instruction may proceed so slowly that pupil interest is destroyed, or it may advance so rapidly that many pupils fail to master even the minimum essential skills.

The third type of test, the *measurement test*, is the type toward which most of the discussion in this book is directed. This test is difficult in that it purports to give exact measurement of each pupil's achievement during the school year, during the semester, or at the end of a unit of teaching. This test, if it is the informal objective type, has a 50-percent level of difficulty, that is, the average pupil will answer 50 percent of the items correctly. Also, this test has the items arranged in a power arrangement from easy to difficult, with the first few items easy enough for the slowest pupil and the last items too difficult for the brightest. This arrangement permits the teacher to establish the point of maximum achievement, or the ceiling, for each pupil in the class.

BALANCED TEST PROGRAM

Since the purposes for testing and the objectives of instruction vary, it is readily apparent that the types of tests used in measuring achievement must also vary. There is no one best type of test. The pertinent question in selecting the best type of test in a specific instance is: "Best for what purpose?" What is to be measured and what the measurement will be used for will be most important in determining the type of test form to be used. The teacher who relies solely on the essay, the objective, or the performance test has admitted, at least by implication, that his instructional objectives are limited to the one or two types which his preferred test form best measures; certainly he chooses to ignore the direct measurement of any of his other teaching objectives. Effective, well-rounded instruction demands that a balanced testing program be used for adequate assessment of the varied instructional objectives.

STRENGTHS AND WEAKNESSES OF VARIOUS TEST FORMS

As will subsequently be pointed out, each test form has specific measurement purposes to which it is better adapted than any other form. Ideally, of course, all testing should stress application of knowledge, since the pupil who applies knowledge has obviously mastered it. On the other hand, the pupil who can recall knowledge on a paper-and-pencil test may well fail to apply that knowledge in the solution of problems to which it could be applied. Yet many areas of teaching stress facts, knowledges, and understandings which lay the foundation for further learning but for which there is little immediate application. For this type of learning paper-and-pencil tests of the objective or essay type will give the best estimate of learning.

Four types of tests—oral, objective, essay, and performance—are discussed in detail in this book, and the strengths and weaknesses of each are briefly reviewed here.

ORAL EXAMINATIONS

In Fig. 1.1 are listed the major strengths and weaknesses of oral examinations. It is notable that oral examination can give an extensive picture of the depth and scope of a pupil's knowledge. But in order to do so, sufficient time must be devoted to the examination and the questions must be carefully prepared ahead of time in order to give an adequate sample of the areas covered. The most significant weakness of the oral examination is that it takes too much time to administer to typical classes of 25 to 40 pupils, when each examination takes from one-half to one hour to administer. However, if it does not stress measurement too heavily, oral questioning, is extremely valuable as a teaching device and as a means of stimulating pupil participation in class discussion.

STRENGTHS	WEAKNESSES

ORAL

STRENGTHS	WEAKNESSES
1. Gives extensive measurement.	1. Is too time-consuming.
2. Is useful as an instructional device.	2. Results in poor pupil performance due to lack of practice.
3. Permits teacher to give cues to elicit desired responses.	3. Provides limited sample unless pupils are tested individually.
4. Improves test rapport for pupils who fear written examinations.	4. Is frequently poorly planned.
	5. Is not subject to refinement.
	6. Gives poor comparative evaluation of pupils.

OBJECTIVE

STRENGTHS	WEAKNESSES
1. Gives an extensive test sample.	1. Frequently neglects measurement of higher thought processes.
2. Can be made highly reliable.	2. Overemphasizes rote learning.
3. Can be graded objectively and quickly.	3. Promotes poor study habits.
4. Eliminates bluffing.	4. Encourages guessing.
5. Can be subjected to item analysis and further refinement.	5. Is difficult to prepare.
6. Can be adapted to several teaching objectives.	6. Costs more than essay to prepare and reproduce.
7. Can be made highly valid for some teaching objectives.	

ESSAY

STRENGTHS	WEAKNESSES
1. Is applicable to measurement of writing, organizational ability, and creativeness.	1. Gives a limited test sample.
	2. Is difficult to grade.
2. Is easy to construct.	3. Favors the verbally inclined student.
3. Promotes proper type of study.	4. Has low reliability.
4. Is adaptable to several subject fields.	5. Encourages bluffing.

PERFORMANCE

STRENGTHS	WEAKNESSES
1. Stresses application of knowledge.	1. Is not adaptable to many fields of learning.
2. Can be used as a learning device.	
3. May give a truer achievement picture for the verbally handicapped pupil.	2. Is difficult to construct.
	3. Is often difficult to grade.
4. Measures some skills and abstract abilities not measured by other conventional test forms.	4. Is often time-consuming.

FIG. 1.1. *Strengths and Weaknesses of Various Test Forms.*

OBJECTIVE TESTS

The objective test in its various forms is the most frequently used in American public schools. In fact, it is often used to measure types of learning for which it is ill-fitted. The strengths and weaknesses of this test form are presented in Fig. 1.1. The most important strength of the objective test is that it permits reliable measurement of an extensive sample of factual material. However, it is difficult to construct objective tests which measure such types of learning as complex understandings, creativity, attitude changes, and problem-solving. Unless the teacher is skilled in test construction, he should avoid attempting to measure these learnings objectively.

ESSAY TESTS

The traditional bulwark of the teacher's testing repertoire has been the essay test, although it has fallen into some disrepute during the emphasis in recent years on the scientific method and the collection of objective data implied by such a method. Nevertheless, it is still true in education that the object of instruction, the pupil, retains his complexity and is characterized by many intangible traits and changes which are almost impossible to objectify, classify, and count. Until the time comes when test experts are able to isolate, define, and classify all the myriad changes which take place in pupils, we shall of necessity continue to rely on the essay test for evaluation of such changes.

Figure 1.1 emphasizes the specific strengths and weaknesses of the essay test form. It is notable that this test form is strong where the objective test is weak, that is, it measures the nonstructured types of learning: problem-solving, creative thinking, writing, and organizational ability. It is inadequate for sampling a great breadth of knowledge, and it is extremely unreliable because of subjective grading.

PERFORMANCE TESTS

Ultimately, of course, most teaching aims to improve pupil performance in a variety of situations by developing skills, knowledges, and understandings which can be successfully applied in the mundane affairs of life. Thus it is prudent, whenever possible, to check achievement by evaluating it in actual performance situations. When the major objectives of the subject fields are oriented toward promoting immediate changes in specified types of performance, the performance test is applicable. This is true of such fields as vocational arts, dramatics, and speech. In these fields primary emphasis in measurement should be placed on performance. Figure 1.1 indicates that the strength of the performance test lies in its ability to garner information about the application of classroom learnings in actual job performance. The most significant weakness of this test form is that it is difficult to adapt to fields in which immediate application of learning may not be the major objective.

SELECTION OF TEACHING OBJECTIVES

Every teacher should have in mind a number of specific and general educational objectives, consistent with his over-all educational philosophy, toward which his instruction is directed. These objectives should be stated in writing, and they should be known and understood by all pupils in his classroom. With such a framework for classroom instruction, it is apparent to both the teacher and his pupils where the class is heading, and measurement need be taken only to ascertain the extent of each pupil's accomplishment of the anticipated objectives. Although each teacher certainly has in mind some of the things which he is attempting to do, many do not have these aims well enough formulated that they can write them down, and some become upset when it is suggested that they should formulate written philosophy and objectives. These people are confused teachers, for they have no *modus operandi*—they "can't see the forest for the trees," so to speak. In such cases some of the general statements of objectives which have been formulated in the past by educators and philosophers offer some framework so that the teacher can begin to see where his classroom efforts fit into the total picture.

GENERAL STATEMENTS OF OBJECTIVES

Until about the beginning of the twentieth century there were few statements of educational objectives. Perhaps this was true because in the nineteenth century educational efforts were directed toward the immediately practical task of establishing an unbroken system of public schools, elementary through university. In any case, by 1900 elementary schools had achieved their present graded form, exclusive of the junior high school organization, and the three R's had gained respect. In contrast, the secondary school, with its limited enrollment, was engaged chiefly with the more restricted objective of preparing all of its pupils for college entrance. There were, however, a few perceptive men, among them Francis Parker and Charles Eliot, who foresaw the complexities which changing social and economic conditions would impose on education. These men began to speak of new educational objectives and to point to the school's responsibility for handling individual differences and for promoting social adjustment. They concerned themselves largely with the changes necessary to achieve the new objectives, an interest that resulted in the introduction of elective subjects at secondary and college levels and of teacher-pupil planning at the elementary level. But with these innovations in American education came confusion and lack of concensus concerning classroom objectives. Social and economic changes, rather than alleviating this confusion, have compounded it. Technology, the depression, the two world wars, the tremendous upsurge in school enrollment have forced continuous change in education at all levels from the nursery school through the university.

In an effort to give directions to secondary education, in 1917 the Commission on the Reorganization of Secondary Education listed seven general objectives of education which later came to be called the Seven Cardinal Objectives of Secondary Education. There have been numerous other excellent statements of general educational objectives, notable among which are those of the Educational Policies Commission. Although general statements of objectives have value in directing the total school program, they do not serve the needs of the individual classroom teacher unless they are broken down into specifics and adapted to his situation. In fact, Russia, France, or England would find most of the general objectives of American education as acceptable in their educational systems as they are in the United States. Such lists of objectives, however, should be useful as a point of reference to an individual teacher, provided that he do some thinking about his own situation and that he formulate specific and general teaching objectives to direct his own classroom efforts.

In formulating his objectives the teacher must keep in mind several principles. First, the objectives must not run counter to the interests of the community which supports his school. Obviously, the objectives of the school must be consistent with its supporting society or the support will disintegrate. Second, the objectives must be realistic so that the pupils will be capable of achieving them. It makes as much sense to shoot at the moon with a popgun as to expect a pupil with an IQ of 70 to master algebra. Third, the objectives must be adaptable to instruction. Some objectives can be achieved most effectively through means other than classroom instruction. If this is the case, such objectives might be inappropriate. Fourth, the objectives must be acceptable to the pupils themselves. Because most objectives purport to change pupils in some way, it is probable that those pupils should have some part in formulating the objectives. It is certain that they should be familiar with the objectives and that they accept them as worthy goals; otherwise little progress toward the achievement of the objectives will result.

TERMS OF STATEMENTS

Educational objectives have as their purpose behavioral changes in pupils; thus they should be stated in terms of the changes which the teacher hopes to make. Classroom objectives may be either long- or short-range. For example, a long-range objective which most teachers may have is that of developing the pupil's skill in reading. A short-range objective which a teacher might have is that of having pupils memorize the multiplication tables. Most educational objectives can be classified under the following headings: (1) skills, (2) knowledges, (3) habits, (4) attitudes, (5) activities, (6) appreciation, (7) interest, (8) concepts, (9) achievements, (10) understandings, (11) adjustments, and (12) applications. The categories which are used most often are those of knowledges, skills, and understandings. Objectives should not be stated in such a general way that they are vague nor in such a specific way that they are fragmentary. Also, the objectives should not overlap. Those objectives which are similar should be grouped together so that they are easily understood. Because all objectives do not have the same value, it would be wise to assign numerical weights to each to indicate the emphasis to be given each objective. This emphasis, of course, is particularly important when the evaluation of the pupil's achievement is made.

USE OF OBJECTIVES IN MEASUREMENT

In measurement the instructional objectives serve the dual purposes of determining the choice of test form and the type and number of items which should be included. Actually the progress to be measured in the achievement of objectives and the content areas or subject matter topics which have been taught are the two elements from which the outline of a good test is constructed. For convenience and for ease in assigning relative weights to various sections of the test, the objectives and content areas should be organized in a table of specifications. The construction of a table of specifications is discussed in detail in Chapter 2 and an example of such a table is given in Fig. 2.1. Test items should not be written, however, until the teacher has listed both the objectives and the content areas to be measured and has decided how much emphasis will be placed on each. This procedure helps the teacher to avoid the familiar pitfall of weighting his tests heavily with items from the most recently studied topics or from those areas which he remembers at random, and thereby fail to emphasize some of the most important areas stressed during the semester or year of instruction. Pupils may then justifiably complain that the test was unfair and that their grades do not give a true picture of their achievement in the course.

GENERAL AND SPECIFIC OBJECTIVES

In preparing tests, teachers often forget that achievement applies to all teaching objectives and that the measurement of achievement need not emphasize only knowledge of subject matter. Achievement applies to social adjustments, to the acquirement of interests, attitudes, and appreciations, as well as to the learning of facts; and the specific and general teaching objectives form the blueprint for proper measurement of all such learnings. It is also true that pupil achievement is never a static thing. The pupil achieves many different things each day during his school experience, and any one measurement of a class's achievement of the teaching objectives gives a fixed picture which (assuming a valid instrument and reasonable testing skill) is true of that class only at that time. The constant change in pupil achievement necessitates continuous, comprehensive evaluation; "one-shot" measurement resulting from a single final examination gives an extremely limited view.

There are several approaches to the actual construction of general and specific classroom objectives. Some curriculum experts recommend that the general objectives be stated first, followed by a statement of the specific classroom objectives. The opposite approach—the statement of specifics first, followed by general—is recommended by others. The latter approach has been found to be successful more often than the former approach. A procedure which works well in orienting teachers to their particular contribution to the general school objectives is to have them first of all state 25 to 30 very specific classroom objectives which they have. These specific objectives can then be consolidated by combining the statements for several subject fields, e.g., language arts with social studies, or mathematics with science, to form 15 to 20 general statements. Finally these lists of objectives can be combined into one general list of about 10 to 15 objectives which encompass all the original statements of specific objectives. In this method of formulating objectives, each objective in each subject field is one of the bricks with which the completed house of general objectives is built. Thus each teacher is aware of his anticipated contribution, as well as that of others, to the over-all educational aim of his school. Conversely, the failure of any teacher to achieve with his class the specific objectives which he has outlined will weaken the general structure by leaving students with educational gaps which must be bridged in other classes if the total objective is to be achieved.

SUGGESTED READINGS

AHMANN, J. STANLEY, MARVIN D. GLOCK, and HELEN L. WARDEBERG, *Evaluating Elementary School Pupils*, Boston, Allyn and Bacon, 1960, 435 pp.
This is a particularly useful book for the elementary school teacher. Chapters 2 and 3 include excellent discussions of the methods used in evaluation and have suggestions for translating educational objectives into measurable form.

BRADFIELD, JAMES M., and H. STEWART MOREDOCK, *Measurement and Evaluation in Education*, New York, Macmillan, 1957, 509 pp.
This is a general book in measurement. Chapter 2 contains a most helpful discussion of the ways in which teachers may state their instructional aims so that they can be readily measured. Chapter 3, although somewhat technical, includes a valuable discussion of the merits of a variety of measurement instruments and techniques.

FURST, EDWARD J., *Constructing Evaluation Instruments*, New York, Longmans, Green, Courtesy McKay, 1958, 334 pp.
The first two chapters of this book give extensive discussion, with examples, of the various types of learning outcomes. There are also helpful suggestions for stating the various types of educational objectives in measurable form.

REMMERS, H. H., and N. L. GAGE, *Educational Measurement and Evaluation*, rev. ed., New York, Harper, 1955, 650 pp.
This is an excellent book covering the entire field of measurement. The first section of the book is devoted to achievement testing, and Chapter 2 includes excellent discussion of instructional objectives.

CHAPTER 2 *Planning measurement instruments*

The construction of a good test does not happen by chance. A good test cannot result from a haphazard approach, but when extensive thought, planning, and work are involved in the preparation, a good test inevitably results. At least three steps are essential in the development of a high-quality testing instrument: (1) planning the test, (2) constructing the test, and (3) evaluating the test.

This chapter is devoted to a discussion of the most important steps which should be followed in planning the test before the actual construction of the instrument is undertaken. The construction and evaluation of tests are discussed in subsequent chapters.

PLANNING THE TEST

Considerable planning is necessary before type of testing instrument can be selected. The objectives to be measured ultimately dictate the kind of test selected, although the purpose to which the measurement will be put is a second important consideration. The objectives might require the use of any of the four test types mentioned by Linquist: (1) the identical-elements test, (2) the related-behavior test, (3) the verbalized-behavior test, or (4) the knowledge test.[1] Several examples will clarify this point. If the objective is to measure performance in reading, a reading rate and comprehension test in which the examinee actually undertakes the task being measured (an identical-elements test) would be more valid than a lengthy speed test of objective items. Related-behavior tests in which actual job conditions are simulated would be most desirable if the objective were to predict from measurement future success in a complex job situation where actual tryout would be costly or unfeasible. In instances where behavior in a complex sociopersonal relationship is to be measured, a problem may be described and the examinee asked to verbalize his solution to the problem.

Some objectives cannot be measured immediately by a test. For example, an objective of a civics or American government class might be to stimulate pupils to vote in elections when they reach voting age. Since long-range follow-up into adult life would give the only true measure of such an objective, the teacher must rely either upon verbalized-response measurement or upon observation of pupil behavior in school elections. On the other hand, verbalized response to a question asking pupils to indicate their reading preferences would certainly be a less valid measure of reading preference than teacher observation of the pupils' free reading choices. Most often the first three types of tests mentioned above are avoided and the knowledge test used, on the assumption that possession of knowledge and the application of it are highly correlated. The conventional objective- and essay-type tests are best adapted for the measurement of knowledges.

Sometimes specific facts are taught as steppingstones to the development of broad generalizations and concepts. In such cases the facts themselves may be forgotten quickly, but the generalizations may represent long-term gains. However, it is permissible to use a content test to get an immediate measure of factual knowledge as a basis for proceeding to the more important concepts. Standardized achievement tests often emphasize this detailed factual content, but

[1] E. F. Linquist (ed.), *Educational Measurement*, Washington, D.C., American Council on Education, 1941, pp. 146–151.

high-level performance on such tests should not cause the teacher to become complacent and fail to achieve the further objectives which lie beyond the facts.

TABLE OF SPECIFICATIONS

A high-quality informal objective test is one planned from an outline based on the teaching objectives and the class content. Perhaps the best way to insure adequate measurement of all the important areas is to construct a test-specification chart. Such a chart is easily made if the teacher has his objectives clearly in mind. In order that we might follow the process of constructing a test-specification chart, let us assume that a high school chemistry teacher has been teaching the following six content areas and that he wishes to measure his effectiveness:

1. The theory of atomic structure.
2. The laws of chemical combination.
3. Behavior of chemical elements in solution.
4. Oxidation-reduction of chemical elements.
5. Atomic structure and chemical behavior of the elements in the periodic table.
6. Physical and chemical properties of such common elements as hydrogen and oxygen and their compounds.

In teaching these six content areas he has had the following five teaching objectives in mind:

1. Recall of important information.
2. Understanding of the structure of chemical elements and their behavior in compounds.
3. Application of the laws of chemical behavior in simple predictions.
4. Application of mathematical principles to chemical change.
5. Ability to use the scientific method.

The table of specifications for this teacher's tests, then, will have as its basis the six content areas and the five objectives. Figure 2.1

shows the completed table of specifications. When the objectives are listed in the left-hand column and the content areas across the top, the table gives a convenient framework to insure adequate test coverage of all important points. The totals in the right-hand column show the number of test items to be used in measuring each objec-

| Teaching Objectives | Number of Items | | | | | | |
| | Content Areas | | | | | | |
	1	2	3	4	5	6	Total
1. Recall of important information	4	3	4	5	5	5	26
2. Understanding of the structure of chemical elements and their behavior in compounds	5	5	5	3	0	5	23
3. Application of the laws of chemical behavior in simple predictions	3	5	3	5	5	5	26
4. Application of mathematical principles to chemical change	3	3	3	5	0	5	19
5. Ability to use the scientific method	5	5	5	3	3	3	24
Total	20	21	20	21	13	23	118

Fig. 2.1. *Table of Specifications for a Chemistry Test.*

tive. Similarly the totals at the bottom of the table show the number of items to be used in measuring each content area. It is customary with objective tests to allow one score point for each test item; therefore the point value for items need not be included in the table of specifications unless an essay test is planned.

Objectives such as No. 5, "ability to use the scientific method," can be measured more readily by essay or performance tests than by objective tests, and the teacher might decide either to supplement the objective test with essay questions or to give an essay or performance test later. In any case, the table of specifications is just as important in planning other test forms as in planning the informal objective test.

GENERAL PRINCIPLES OF TEST CONSTRUCTION

The table of specifications is the blueprint from which a type of test may be selected and actual test construction may proceed. However, at this point it is appropriate to enumerate several principles of general test construction which should be followed to insure a high-quality measuring instrument.

1. *The test should be long enough to be valid and reliable but short enough to be usable.* The length necessary to insure valid measurement depends upon the number and complexity of the objectives being measured. One or two objectives might conceivably have a highly valid measurement with a very short test. Reliability, however, is related more directly to the length of a test than to the objectives, and increasing the length of a test increases its reliability. This statement assumes, though, that those items which are added to lengthen the test are of equal quality to the items in the rest of the test. Poorly written items added solely to lengthen a test may have the effect of actually decreasing the reliability of the instrument. There is also a point of diminishing returns where lengthening the test, even with excellent test items, will lower reliability since variable fatigue of the examinees affects the test results. The usability of the test demands that it be short enough to be administered within the normal division of the school day—the 45–55 minute period in the high school and a 30–45-minute period in the elementary school. The time which a test will take can be estimated from the fact that an average high school pupil can complete two typical multiple-choice items or three typical true-false items per minute. Pupils at higher or lower grade levels can complete slightly more or fewer items, respectively. Thus the question of test length forces the test-maker to compromise between the considerations of validity, reliability, and usability.

Whether the test is a speed or a power test may also influence its length, because with speed tests the pupil ceiling is in terms of number of items completed successfully during the time allowed, whereas the power test has the ceiling in terms of difficulty of items. A speed test, if it has a ceiling for all students, will have to include more items than any pupil can complete within the time limit. The power test, however, need not have as many items since pupils will cease to answer the items correctly before they reach the end of the test or before the time elapses.

2. *A measurement test should be a power test, wherein the first few items are simple enough for all students to answer.* This principle permits the pupil to start the test with a better test psychology in that he immediately experiences success which gives him some security. Occasionally a student has such poor test psychology that he has major test blocks which prevent his performing at his normal level and cause him to fail on items which he could answer were he not in a test situation. Open-book tests and optional test questions perform somewhat the same function of setting the psychological stage for optimum test performance. Open-book tests may have the additional value of helping the pupil collect additional information while taking the test, although this gain will be negligible. Alternate questions in an essay test have the effect of increasing the test sample for the class, but they actually lower reliability and probably contribute little to the measurement function of the test. Neither open-book tests nor optional questions make major changes in the test standings of a group of examinees.

3. *The test should be designed in such a way that reading rate and comprehension do not unduly influence the test scores.* A rapid reader may complete most of the items in an extremely long test, while a better student in the subject may complete only half of the items and get a lower score, although he could have answered all of the items correctly had he been given sufficient time. In such a case reading speed and not subject matter competence is measured. To get an accurate measurement of the achievement of each pupil, it is necessary to write the items in language simple enough to allow slow readers to understand the questions, and to allot sufficient time

for the test so that slow readers have time to respond to all the questions for which they know the answers. There are, of course, some instances when the teacher wishes to measure reading rate and comprehension as a part of the test. In these cases more difficult language will be used, and the time limit will be shortened so that only the fastest readers can complete the test.

4. *A test should generally consist of no more than two or three types of items, and all the items of one type should be included in one section.* For example, a test might include both true-false and multiple-choice or matching items, but all of the true-false items should be in one section and not interspersed throughout the test. If numerous teaching objectives are being measured and if they require the use of a number of different kinds of test items, it is better to give several different tests at different times, instead of forcing the pupil to change his mind-set too many times during one test by including in it four or five different kinds of items.

5. *The test items should be clear and concise,* without the confusion of unnecessary words or unusual vocabulary. A test in which little care has been taken with the wording of questions can actually interfere with measurement, as inaccurate wording often prevents the pupil from understanding the questions asked, and he may thus be unable to answer even those questions to which he otherwise would have a ready answer. The aim of the test-maker is to prepare an instrument which will measure the pupil's attainment of the objectives as accurately as possible. With the objective-type test it is particularly important that there be no clues to the correct answers other than the meaning of the questions. Since the pupil who has taken many objective tests tends to become "test-wise" and take advantage of the slightest clue in the grammar or wording of items, his score may represent an invalid measure of teaching objectives, and instead be a measure of his adeptness at second-guessing the instructor.

The task of the test-maker is alleviated if he can write several test items each time he plans a lesson. This is particularly helpful if objective tests are to be used, since it gives the teacher a backlog of items from which to choose when the tests are actually prepared. For purposes of filing and keeping items it is helpful to write each item on a 3×5 file card. If the items are written on this type of card and kept, information from an item analysis after the item has been used can be entered on the card. Also it is possible to file items by objective or topic. Such an extensive file may be built up that it would be possible to construct several alternate forms measuring the same objectives and having approximately the same difficulty level without duplicating any of the test items. With such a file teachers may use test items several times without having to repeat an entire test.

6. *The test directions should be clear and explicit.* When the pupil reads the directions, he should have no doubt in his mind as to the kind of answers he is to give nor the way in which he is to indicate his responses. In objective tests if a correction formula is to be used for scoring, the directions should indicate it to the pupil.

7. *The test items should have a simple method of indicating responses,* and they should be easy to score. The following directions and response method have been found effective with true-false tests for high school and college students:

TRUE-FALSE EXAMINATION

Directions: In the following true-false test cross out the T if the item is correct; cross out the F if the item is incorrect.

T F   1. The curriculum of the medieval university evolved from the Roman Trivium and Quadrivium.

When this method of indicating responses is used for true-false items, scoring can be facilitated by preparing a cardboard scoring key which may be placed over the test paper to mark the incorrect responses.

The following examples include directions which have been found effective with multiple-choice and matching tests.

With slight modifications, the directions for the matching text below can fit most matching lists. For example, if men are to be listed in Column I and matched with identifying phrases from Column II, the directions could read: "In the parentheses preceding each man's name in Column I place the letter of the phrase from Column II which identifies the man."

Multiple-Choice Examination

Directions: In the blank before each item place the letter which identifies the correct response.

_____ 1. The most reliable measure of variability of a group of test scores is the:
  A. range
  B. quartile deviation
  C. standard deviation
  D. semi-interquartile range
  E. frequency distribution

Matching Examination

Directions: In the parentheses preceding each item in Column I put the letter of the choice from Column II which completes or identifies the item.

Column I	Column II
( ) 1.	a.
( ) 2.	b.
( ) 3.	c.
( ) 4.	d.
( ) 5.	e.
	f.
	g.
	h.

In all objective forms lower elementary grade children should be given, in addition to the directions, examples of the method of indicating their responses.

8. *The test should be typed and reproduced by ditto or mimeograph* so that each pupil can have a copy. Because in preparing stencils it is easy to make typographical errors, the teacher should proofread the stencils before the test is run off; errors may change the entire meaning of some of the important test items.

9. *The test should be appropriate to the ability and age level of the pupils.* Common sense on the part of the teacher will determine the relative difficulty which a test should have. Almost any teacher could construct a test in his field which would be so difficult that none of his pupils could succeed. He could also construct such an easy test that all of his pupils would get high scores. It is therefore

necessary that the teacher know his pupils well enough that he can fit the difficulty of the test to their age and abilities. Beginning teachers often fail in this respect. For example, one beginning teacher of a high school freshman class in general science gave one of his first tests, which was to be used for the purpose of assigning marks on the report cards that were to go home to the parents. The poor test results were a severe shock to this teacher, for he felt that his teaching had been excellent and that all of his pupils should have been able to answer most of the questions. Actually the best pupils answered correctly fewer than half the questions, whereas the poorest experienced virtually no success. Undoubtedly both poor instruction and poor test construction were responsible for the low test scores.

SUGGESTED READINGS

AHMANN, J. STANLEY, MARVIN D. GLOCK, and HELEN L. WARDEBERG, *Evaluating Elementary School Pupils*, Boston, Allyn and Bacon, 1960, 435 pp.
     Chapter 13 includes suggestions and examples for evaluating the content areas of a variety of subject fields.

REMMERS, H. H., N. L. GAGE, and J. FRANCIS RUMMEL, A *Practical Introduction to Measurement and Evaluation*, New York, Harper, 1960, 370 pp.
     Chapter 8, in addition to giving an excellent statement of how to select the evaluation device, has extremely good discussion, suggestions, and examples for all the important types of teacher-made tests. This chapter is a useful guide for helping teachers to improve their testing.

TRAVERS, ROBERT M. W., *How to Make Achievement Tests*, New York, Odyssey, 1949, 180 pp.
     This book gives one of the best considerations of the construction of the objective-test form, although it has insufficient discussion of the other important test forms. Chapter 2 deals with the planning and construction of the test outline.

WOOD, DOROTHY ADKINS, *Test Construction*, Columbus, Ohio, Merrill, 1960, 134 pp.
     The entire book deals specifically with teacher-made tests, and Chapter 6 gives helpful suggestions for planning objective tests, as well as several examples of test outlines.

CHAPTER 3

Construction and use of informal objective tests

A good table of specifications forms the outline from which a test can be constructed, but it does not include the actual ideas from which items are written. The writing of good objective-test items is a difficult, creative task, and the professional item-writer who works on standardized tests may feel that he has had a productive day if he has written from five to fifteen acceptable achievement-test items. This chapter is devoted to the rules for writing acceptable items, with examples of good and bad items, and to discussion of the advantages and weaknesses of some of the test forms.

Rules in themselves, however, do not guarantee good items. For a technically correct item may not include an important idea for measuring anything worthwhile. In order to be a successful item-writer, a teacher should have the following qualifications:

1. He must have thorough mastery of his subject matter.
2. He must possess a rational and well-developed set of educational objectives.
3. He must understand, psychologically and educationally, the individuals for whom the test is intended.

4. He must be a master of verbal communication.
5. He must be skilled in handling special techniques of item-writing, in inventing situations which require exactly the right knowledge of the examinees.

Given the above prerequisites for item-writing, rules and suggestions for constructing the following test forms will be discussed: (1) short-answer form, (2) alternate-response form, (3) multiple-choice form, and (4) matching form.

SHORT-ANSWER FORM

The short-answer form may include questions, incomplete sentences, definitions, or identification items. This form is particularly well adapted to the measurement of factual recall, and it has the advantage over true-false and multiple-choice items that the student cannot guess the correct response unless the item has been poorly constructed and includes clues. The following examples show each short-answer variety.

1. QUESTION:
   What is the technical name for nearsightedness?   (_____)

2. INCOMPLETE SENTENCE:
   The name of the first man to sail around the world
   was (_____).   (_____)

3. DEFINITION:
   Define the median: (_____
   _____)

4. IDENTIFICATION:
   Identify the part of speech for each word underlined in the sentence below.
   English common law forms the basis for the American legal system.   (_____)

RULES FOR CONSTRUCTION

Short-answer tests have a wide range of applicability in measuring factual recall in many subject fields, provided the items are carefully constructed and the rules are observed. The most important rules to be followed in the construction of this type of test are given below.

1. *Only significant words should be omitted in incomplete-statement items.* Otherwise the item will not make an important contribution to the measurement of the intended objective.

EXAMPLE:

> The law of inertia states that a body at rest tends to remain at rest, and a body in motion tends to remain in motion.

Leaving out the word *inertia* would check the pupil's recognition of the law and his recall of the name of the law, whereas leaving out the two *at rest* phrases and the two *in motion* phrases would test either rote memory or understanding of the law. Leaving out such words as *law* and *body* would give little important measurement result.

2. *When omitting words to make an incomplete statement, enough clues should be left so that the pupil who knows the answer can supply the correct response.*

EXAMPLE:

> In an internal-combustion engine the (_____)
> converts the straight-line motion of the pistons into
> the circular motion of the drive shaft.   crankshaft

In this example the word *piston* could also be omitted without overmutilating the statement; but if the words *drive shaft* were omitted, there might be a variety of correct responses, e.g., *flywheel, wheels, differential gears.*

3. *Grammatical clues to the correct answer should be avoided.* If teachers include grammatical clues in their questions, "test-wise" pupils may answer a number of the questions correctly because they find the clues rather than because they know the answers.

FAULTY EXAMPLE

> An engine which uses explosive gas as its
> energy source is called an (_____)
> engine.   internal-combustion

If this item were rephrased as a question to read as follows, it would be a much better item.

What is an engine which uses explosive gas as its energy source called?

4. *Overmutilated statements should be avoided.* When too many blanks are left, an incomplete statement has no meaning. It is much better to include several statements with fewer blanks in each than to mutilate one important statement to the extent that it ceases to have an important measurement function.

FAULTY EXAMPLE:

The (_____) is obtained by dividing the   quotient
(_____) by the (_____).   dividend
                                                    divisor

This statement becomes a good statement when the word *quotient* is retained in the first blank so that the item reads: "The quotient is obtained by dividing the (_____) by the (_____)."

5. *Blanks should be kept uniform in length so that the pupil is not given the unnecessary clues of a short blank for a short response and a long blank for a long response.* Be certain, however, to include sufficient space for the longest response.

EXAMPLE:

The Gregorian calendar contains (_____)   <u>365</u>
days and is based on astronomical calculation of   <u>around the sun</u>
the earth's orbit (_____).

The two blanks in the right-hand column in which these responses are to be written are long enough to accommodate the longer response.

6. *One point should be allowed for each blank.* Therefore each word or phrase omitted must be of comparable importance and difficulty. The total raw score on the test is based on the total number of blanks included and not on the number of items or statements included.

7. *Blanks should be arranged in a manner convenient to score.* For upper-grade and secondary pupils it is best to follow the form illustrated below and have the responses entered in the blanks in either the right-hand or the left-hand column of the page. Then a

previously prepared cardboard key can be placed next to the answer columns for easy scoring.

EXAMPLE:

What part of speech shows action or state of being?   _____

8. When the question form is used, *questions should be explicit enough to evoke the correct type of response.* The only reason for a pupil's failure on an item should be his lack of recall or knowledge, not his failure to understand the question. It is also essential that the questions be so constructed that there can be only one possible answer in the form of a word, phrase, or number. If there is more than one correct answer, the scoring will be subjective and extremely difficult, as each answer will have to be judged on its relative correctness.

EXAMPLE:

What was the population of Japan in 1961?   _____

9. *Verbatim quotes from the textbook should be avoided.* Short-answer tests tend to stress rote memory, and verbatim quoting further emphasizes this weakness. Rephrasing important textbook statements serves the additional purpose of checking the pupil's understanding.

10. *A scoring key which contains all acceptable answers should be prepared.* Such a key facilitates scoring. But occasionally the teacher may construct poor items which have correct answers other than those included on his key. In such cases the teacher must either eliminate the poor items or add the correct responses to the acceptable answers on the key.

WEAKNESSES OF SHORT-ANSWER TESTS

The short-answer test is most effective in measuring recall, but it has several weaknesses. First, it is extremely difficult to construct items which call for only one correct answer. If too many clues are given in the item, most of the pupils will answer it correctly, but the item will then be too easy to give any measurement. If too few clues are given, there may be a great variety of answers due to the pupils' failure to understand the type of response desired. Here again measurement is limited. Second, completion-type items stress rote recall and encourage pupils to spend their time memorizing trivial details rather than seeking important understandings. Third, completion items are somewhat unrealistic since life problems generally offer a variety of possible solutions rather than one "key-word" solution.

ALTERNATE-RESPONSE FORM

The alternate-response form generally consists of a statement to be judged true or false. Of course, since the true-false item offers only two alternatives, the element of chance may be a large factor in the correct response of the pupil. If the pupil were to flip a coin and answer the item true for heads or false for tails, he would have one chance out of two of answering the item correctly. Thus the items have to be constructed carefully and without unnecessary clues which might increase the pupil's guessing success. If the true-false test is carefully constructed and is long enough to be valid and reliable, it can be a very good instrument for measuring both factual knowledge and understanding of important concepts.

Although the most common form for alternate-response items is that of a direct statement which is to be judged true or false, there are several variations, among which are the following:

1. The pressure in a fixed quantity of a gas varies directly as its volume if the temperature remains constant.   T F
2. Does a ripsaw have larger teeth than a crosscut saw?
3. *Make every false statement true by suggesting a substitute for the underlined word.*

   The use of steam revolutionized transportation in the seventeenth century.   ————

4. The volume of a mass of gas
   a. tends to increase as the temperature increases.   T F
   b. tends to increase as the pressure increases.   T F
   c. may be held constant by increasing pressure and decreasing temperature   T F
   d. may be reduced by increasing pressure and decreasing temperature   T F

RULES FOR CONSTRUCTION

1. *Each statement should be entirely true or entirely false.* It is not uncommon to find true-false statements consisting of several clauses, with an introductory clause which is true and a subsequent, qualifying clause which is not true.

FAULTY EXAMPLE:
> Dogs are mammals, and they are the most intelligent animals with the exception of man.

Such a statement may confuse the student because it is half true and half false. If the statement were changed to "The dog is the most intelligent animal," it would be a clear-cut false statement.

2. *Trivial details should not make a statement false.* A statement should, instead, be a fundamentally false idea.

FAULTY EXAMPLE:
> Columbus first landed in the Caribbean Islands in 1493.

This is a poor statement because 1493 does not represent enough change in the date. The statement might better read, "Columbus discovered America in 1510." In this case the statement is fundamentally false because Columbus did not discover America and 1510 is a date in the century after his first landing in the new world.

3. *Statement should be concise without more elaboration than is necessary to give clear meaning.* Furthermore, it is desirable to use words having precise meaning rather than words which approximate the desired meanings.

EXAMPLE:
> The Egyptians had a polytheist type of religion.

Lengthening the statement in the following ambiguous manner decreases its measurement value: "The people who inhabited the Nile Valley two thousand years before the birth of Christ worshiped numerous gods, the most important of whom were Seth, the god of evil, and Osiris, the god of good."

4. *Exact statements should not be quoted from the textbook.* Rather it is best to modify the wording in order to defeat the rote learner who can identify the words of the text without understanding them.

5. *Quantitative terms should be used instead of qualitative terms, whenever possible.*

EXAMPLE:
   There have been four Democratic presidents of the United States since World War I.

If the word *several* were substituted for the word *four* in the statement above, it would become a qualitative statement which could be given a variety of interpretations. To one person the term *several* may mean two, but to another it may mean thirty.

6. *Specific determiners which give a cue to the answer should be avoided.*

EXAMPLE:
   Women have a longer life-span than men.

This true statement becomes false when the specific determiner *all* is included so that it reads, "All women have a longer life-span than men." The statement again becomes true, although ambiguous, when cued with the specific determiner *sometimes* to read, "Sometimes women have a longer life-span than men." Statements which begin with *all* or *always* are nearly always false, whereas statements containing the words *sometimes* or *maybe* tend to be true. Furthermore, some test-makers consistently begin false statements with the same phrase and start true statements with another overworked phrase. The meaning of the total statement, and not one word or phrase, should be the only cue to the correct answer.

7. *Negative statements should be avoided.*

FAULTY EXAMPLE:
   Man cannot exist without oxygen.

Although this is a short concise statement, it contains two negatives, *cannot* and *without*. The statement would be much improved if it were rephrased to read, "Man needs oxygen to exist." Negative statements tend to be misread by pupils. They do, however, serve the purpose of giving some measurement of the pupil's reading ability.

8. *When a controversial statement is used, authority should be quoted.* This permits the pupil to judge the correctness or incorrectness of the statement from his knowledge of the authority's stand; otherwise he has to answer on the basis of his own opinion or guess what the opinion of the instructor might be.

EXAMPLE:

> According to President Kennedy, federal aid to public elementary and secondary schools is desirable.

The pupil can answer the statement above correctly if he knows President Kennedy's opinion, thus he is not placed in the quandary of attempting to guess the instructor's opinion.

9. *A pattern of answers should be avoided.* Teachers tend to include more true than false items in their true-false tests; consequently the "test-wise" pupil who knows little about the subject being tested can improve his score by marking true all items about which he was in doubt. Sometimes a test may include a pattern, such as two true, one false, two true, one false, so that it is easy for the student to determine the answers to items which he does not know. To avoid this difficulty the teacher should consciously vary the proportion and arrangement of true items and false items.

WEAKNESSES OF ALTERNATE-RESPONSE TESTS

Perhaps one of the most obvious weaknesses of this form of test is the fact that it encourages pupils to guess. In addition, this type of test is often poorly constructed. The teacher may select most of the items directly from the text, and he often fails to spend sufficient time in planning the test and refining the items. It is a common fault of teachers to include more true statements than false in each of their tests, thus enhancing the pupil's chances of guessing correctly. But in spite of its weaknesses, the alternate-response test can be a valuable measurement aid when it is carefully constructed.

MULTIPLE-CHOICE FORM

The multiple-choice test is considered by most test experts to be the best type of objective test for measuring a variety of educational objectives. The test is versatile, and it requires some discriminatory thinking on the part of the pupil. Multiple-choice items have a premise which consists of an incomplete statement or question followed by several choices which include one correct answer and several distracters. The incomplete statement and the question are the most common multiple-choice forms. The question-type item tends to be somewhat easier than the incomplete statement to understand. Multiple-choice items can be made either very easy or extremely difficult. Increasing the homogeneity of the choices makes an item more difficult. For example, the following item is relatively easy:

What does the term *consistent* mean?
a. Steady.
b. Unsteady.
c. Compatible.
d. Fluid.
e. Changeable.

Changing the choices in the following manner makes the item considerably more difficult:

What does the term *consistent* mean?
a. Steady.
b. Repetitious.
c. Revolving.
d. Compatible.
e. Predictable.

The multiple-choice test is useful for measuring a variety of different types of learnings. The following item measures understanding of the correlation concept:

Which of the following coefficients of correlation has the highest predictive value?
a.   0.85
b.   0.75

   c. −0.30
   d. −0.95
   e.   0.50

The following item measures recall and understanding of a definition:

> Social distance refers to the
>   a. sense of nearness or remoteness with regard to other persons or groups.
>   b. sense of superiority of the members of the in-group toward the out-group.
>   c. role of identification in developing a sense of group remoteness.
>   d. sense of remoteness among members of an in-group.
>   e. role of the in-group in promoting social mobility of its members.

The following item measures ability to think through a process and to note errors:

> In computing the mean of a distribution from grouped data, the sums of the deviations above and below the arbitrary origin were found to be 127 and 189, respectively. The final value for the mean was in error. Which of the following possibilities is likely to have caused the error in computation?
>   a. Failure to note the correct sign in adding the mean of the deviations to the assumed origin.
>   b. Use of an assumed mean higher than the true mean.
>   c. Omission of some of the cases in tabulating the data.
>   d. Division by the wrong number of cases.
>   e. Multiplication by the wrong class-interval value.

The following item measures reasoning ability:

> The egg is to the animal as the seed is to the:
>   a. tree.
>   b. plant.
>   c. soil.
>   d. fruit.
>   e. flower.

The following item measures rote learning:

> In the normal curve what percent of the cases lies within one standard deviation plus and minus the mean?
>   a. 62%.

   b. 68%.
   c. 75%.
   d. 58%.
   e. 34%.

The following item measures ability to select a false response:

> Which one of the following statements concerning John Locke's educational writings is untrue?
>   a. They were published in a book called *Some Thoughts on Education*.
>   b. They debunked the idea that knowledge and ideas are innate
>   c. They supported the *tabula rasa* theory of education.
>   d. They were concerned with the individual differences of pupils.
>   e. They supported the mental-discipline concept.

The multiple-choice test is sometimes varied by making all of the choices correct and requiring the pupil to select the best choice. This modification is extremely difficult to construct and should not be attempted by the teacher who lacks experience in test construction. Another variation occasionally used is that of making all but one of the choices correct and requiring the pupil to select the incorrect one. This type is also difficult to construct, and it has the disadvantage of overemphasizing errors by using a negative approach.

RULES FOR CONSTRUCTION

Sources from which material for writing items may be taken include textbooks, reference works, magazine articles, and lecture notes; but normally the material taken from these sources is not appropriate for an item, but rather is useful in providing ideas which can be adapted to make good test items. In spite of its usefulness as a measuring device, the multiple-choice test item is one of the most difficult of the objective-type items to construct. The rules listed and discussed below indicate some of the pitfalls to be avoided in the construction of items, but they do not insure the writing of good items. Good item-writing calls for ingenuity and considerable effort, as well as adherence to these rules.

1. *The central problem of the item should be stated in the premise so as to make only one choice justifiable.* An item such as the one

below permits too great a range of alternative choices to be useful in measurement.

FAULTY EXAMPLE:
    Ethnic groups are:
        a. artifacts.
        b. cultural groups.
        c. racial groups.
        d. external influences.
        e. language groups.

Because no problem is presented in the premise of the item above, a variety of choices is possible. A statement such as the following is much superior.

EXAMPLE:
    What characteristic best identifies an ethnic group?
        a. Common artifacts.
        b. Shared culture.
        c. Similar racial background.
        d. Common language.
        e. Similar appearance.

2. *All choices in the item should be grammatically consistent.* Each choice should be grammatically correct as an ending for the premise. As many as possible of the words of the item should be included in the premise to avoid repetition in each choice, as well as to help keep the choices brief.

EXAMPLE:
    Why do living organisms need oxygen?
        a. To purify the blood.
        b. To oxidize waste.
        c. To release energy.
        d. To assimilate food.
        e. To fight infection.

3. *The choices should be as brief as possible, and the correct response should be neither consistently longer nor shorter than the incorrect responses.*

EXAMPLE:
    According to the "natural depravity of man" doctrine of medieval religious groups, man was inherently:
        a. good.

    b. evil.
    c. degraded.
    d. unreasonable.
    e. deprived.

4. *A pattern of answers should be avoided.* Teachers tend to make a large number of the correct responses either the first or the last choice. In the process of constructing items, it helps to place the correct choice in the first position, and then when all the items have been constructed, to go back and randomly distribute the correct choices so that each position is used approximately the same number of times.

5. *Negatively stated items should be avoided.*

FAULTY EXAMPLE:
    Which of the following is not a characteristic of the successful group leader?
    a. He defines the group purpose.
    b. He suggests courses of action.
    c. He shares group experiences.
    d. He opposes group interests.
    e. He justifies group actions.

The negative multiple-choice item, just as the negative true-false item, tends to measure reading ability. Poor readers often answer such items incorrectly, even when they know the correct answers.

6. *Authority should be quoted when the item contains controversial opinion.*

EXAMPLE:
    American historians generally agree that the major responsibility for causing World War I lay with:
    a. Germany and Austria.
    b. Germany and Serbia.
    c. Russia and France.
    d. England and France.
    e. Russia and Italy.

If the premise were reworded to read "It is generally agreed that the major responsibility for causing World War I lay with," then there might be several correct answers. For instance, some pupils could argue that German historians generally agree that England and France were responsible. It is unfair to ask the pupil to respond to an opinion item unless he has the reference point of an authority, for he may either disagree with or be unfamiliar with the instructor's opinion.

7. *Ambiguous items should be avoided.* Each item should contain one clearly stated problem, and unnecessary or unusual words should be avoided. The aim of the teacher should be to write items which all pupils can understand. This rule is perhaps violated more frequently than any other rule for constructing multiple-choice items.

FAULTY EXAMPLE:
> When there is an active verb in the sentence, the subject does the acting; and when the verb is passive, the subject is acted upon. Which of the following is passive?
> a. Threw.
> b. Hit.
> c. Ran.
> d. Was hit.
> e. Dropped.

Although the item above is not difficult, it is ambiguous because it deals with two problems. It might better be split into two separate items, one dealing with passive verbs and the other with active verbs.

8. *All choices should be plausible.*

FAULTY EXAMPLE:
> What is the end punctuation for an interrogative sentence?
> a. Exclamation point.
> b. Quotation marks.
> c. Question mark.
> d. Comma.
> e. Semicolon.

If several of the choices are not plausible, the pupil's chances of guessing the correct response are increased. In the five-choice item in the example above, three of the choices are not plausible; therefore the pupil has a 50–50 chance of guessing the correct response. In this instance a true-false item would have been as useful and much easier to construct.

9. *Specific determiners should be avoided.*

FAULTY EXAMPLE:
The part of speech which tells "how," "when," or "where" is an:
   a. noun.
   b. pronoun.
   c. adverb.
   d. conjunction.
   e. verb.

Obviously *adverb* is the correct answer because it is the only choice which begins with a vowel. A grammatical clue such as *a* or *an* preceding a choice aids the pupil who does not know the correct response.

10. *Each item should contain an independent problem which gives no clues to the answers of other items.* Frequently teachers include in a test items which are interrelated and therefore give clues to the answers of several items in the group.

FAULTY EXAMPLE:
When did the American Civil War begin?
   a. 1812.
   b. 1850.
   c. 1861.
   d. 1875.
   e. 1885.

The Morrill Act passed by Congress during the Civil War authorized land grants for the establishment of:
   a. state universities.
   b. agricultural and mechanical colleges.
   c. junior colleges.
   d. medical colleges.
   e. normal schools.

Although the pupil may not know the date of the Civil War, he may know the date of the Morrill Act, which the second item relates to the Civil War; thus he may answer the first item correctly simply because of the clue in the second item.

MATCHING FORM

The matching examination is most useful for measuring recognition and recall. In most subject fields there are specific basic facts or knowledges which the teacher wishes the pupil to retain. For example, in history there are important dates which help the pupil gain a chronological orientation to the entire sweep of historical events. Or in science there are many specific facts which must be retained by the pupil before he can achieve more complex scientific understandings. Matching sets are particularly well adapted to the measurement of such basic facts, and they can be constructed in such a manner that the pupil has virtually no chance of guessing the correct responses.

RULES FOR CONSTRUCTION

1. *Only homogeneous premises and homogeneous responses should be grouped in a single matching set.*

FAULTY EXAMPLE:

For each of the statements on the left, choose the item on the right that goes with it. Put the letter on the line.

_____ grows much wheat	a. Brazil
_____ grows much coffee	b. Canada
_____ capital of Great Britain	c. London
_____ capital of United States	d. New York
	e. Scotland
	f. Washington

BETTER EXAMPLE:

Each city on the left is the capital of one of the countries on the right. Place the letter of the country on the line before its capital city.

_____ Canberra	a. Australia
_____ Edinburgh	b. Canada
_____ London	c. England
_____ Ottawa	d. Irish Free State
	e. Scotland

When several different types of items are included in a single set, the pupil can eliminate inappropriate responses and improve his guessing chances. Matching sets should be presented with their common elements, e.g., organs and their functions, bones and their affiliated muscles, historical events and their dates.

2. *Relatively short lists of responses—not less than five, not more than fifteen—should be used.* When more than fifteen responses are included, the pupil may become confused after being required to read the entire list numerous times. It is best to break up these long sets into several shorter sets.

3. *Premises should be arranged for maximum clarity and convenience to the examinee.* Premises should be in the left-hand column and responses in the right-hand column. For ease in scoring, the answer blanks should precede the premises.

4. *Response options should be arranged alphabetically or chronologically.* When responses are so arranged, the pupil who knows the answers can locate them in the response list in a minimum of time without frequent rereading of the entire list.

5. *Directions should clearly indicate the intended basis for matching.*

EXAMPLE:
    Each agricultural product on the left is an important export of one of the countries on the right. Place the letter of the country on the line before the product it exports.

_____	beef	a. Argentina
_____	coffee	b. Australia
_____	wheat	c. Brazil
_____	wool	d. Canada
		e. England

6. *Providing perfect one-to-one matching between premises and responses should not be attempted.* Vary the location of the correct response, placing it sometimes with its premise, sometimes close to its premise, and sometimes a number of places away from its premise.

7. *All of the choices for each matching set should be included on a single page.* A pupil may become confused if some of the responses appear on another page. In any case his reading task is complicated by such an arrangement.

8. *More responses than premises should be used in a set, or a single*

response should be used to answer several premises. If there is the
same number of premises and responses, pupils will cross out those
which have been used and guess the answers to the remaining
premises.

SUGGESTED READINGS

BEAN, KENNETH LAMONT, *Construction of Educational and Personnel
Tests*, New York, McGraw-Hill, 1953, 231 pp.
  Chapters 3 and 4 are particularly useful in that they include in-
  structions for constructing all the common types of objective items.
  These chapters also provide a variety of examples which are helpful
  to the test-writer.

FURST, EDWARD J., *Constructing Evaluation Instruments*, New York,
Longmans, Green, Courtesy McKay, 1958, 334 pp.
  Chapters 8, 9, 10, and 11 deal extensively with the construction of
  objective-test items. These chapters include helpful suggestions for
  writing the items as well as examples from numerous fields and
  levels of instruction.

GERBERICH, J. RAYMOND, *Specimen Objective Test Items*, New York,
Longmans, Green, Courtesy McKay, 1956, 436 pp.
  This is the most comprehensive consideration of objective-test
  construction. The entire book deals with the topic and would be
  extremely useful to the teacher who is especially interested in
  using the objective test and who wishes to develop professional competence in the construction and use of the form.

WANDT, EDWIN, and GERALD W. BROWN, *Essentials of Educational
Evaluation*, New York, Holt, 1957, 117 pp.
  Chapter 2 is a concise, elementary treatment of the construction
  of objective tests.

WOOD, DOROTHY ADKINS, *Test Construction*, Columbus, Ohio, Merrill,
1960, 134 pp.
  Chapters 5 and 7 deal specifically with the construction of objective-type tests. Suggestions and appropriate examples are included
  for each test type.

CHAPTER 4 *Construction and use of performance tests*

In selecting and training individuals for jobs, and in predicting job performance, paper-and-pencil objective tests are useful; but factors other than those measured by such tests are as significant for success as are the knowledges, skills, and aptitudes necessary for a specific job. Success is difficult to analyze and more difficult to predict. It is apparent, however, that knowledge and the successful application of knowledge in performance do not always correlate highly. It is certain, though, that those who apply knowledge in successful performance have achieved a higher degree of learning than that represented by the mere retentive grasp of knowledge; therefore instruments which measure the performance also give, by inference, measurement of the essential knowledges and skills. Performance tests are the only tests designed specifically to measure directly the actual job performance of pupils; and since successful job performance is an ultimate objective of many courses, the performance test should be used whenever it is adaptable to the area being taught.

This chapter is directed toward helping teachers construct and use performance instruments in those areas in which they are appropriate.

MEASUREMENT APPROACHES

Performance of any task is a complex of many factors, but it includes two measurable aspects: (1) the procedure, skill, or technique, and (2) the product or result. In the case either of the procedure or of the product, a breakdown into the specific factors must precede testing. Then from among those factors the most important must be sampled by the test. Performance-testing is valuable for any subject in which pupils are being taught to follow specific procedures or to create some product. Actually this type of testing is useful in a wide range of subjects, as products are emphasized in English composition, business education, the laboratory sciences, mathematics, industrial arts, and home economics; and procedures are emphasized in several of these fields as well as in the fields of speech, drama, physical education, and music.

Because the product and the procedure may be closely related in the field, for example, in music or drama, the teacher interested in performance measurement may choose to concentrate on the procedure, on the product, or on any combination of the two. After he has decided what he will emphasize, he must select an approach adaptable to his purpose. The three approaches from which he may choose are: (1) identification, (2) simulated conditions, and (3) work samples.

Identification emphasizes knowledge of the product, wherein the pupil is asked to identify the nature and function of various components of the product. For example, in a sewing class in home economics this approach would be used if the girls were asked to identify and explain certain specified parts of the sewing machine. A weakness in this approach is that those who know the parts and their functions may be inept in using the machine.

The *simulated-conditions* approach emphasizes the procedure. With this approach the actual conditions of the job to be measured are duplicated as nearly as possible. For example, many secondary schools are now teaching driver-training; as an aid in teaching the course and measuring the competence of beginning drivers, teachers often use automobile mock-ups which simulate actual driving conditions without the hazard of injury to inexperienced drivers. Similarly in office-practice courses in business education, actual job conditions are simulated for teaching and measurement purposes. Because a number of courses in schools have a general education aim and prepare pupils for a variety of jobs, it is often more difficult to simulate actual job conditions than in the latter illustration. Even in these fields, however, if one were to select a single job to analyze, such a simulated situation could be constructed, although its usefulness would be confined largely to that situation. In certain special areas, such as music, home economics, and industrial arts, very effective use can be made of this approach. If the teacher has initiative, he can successfully adapt this approach to such academic fields as science, mathematics, English, and social science. In fact, the experimental laboratory traditionally used in teaching chemistry is actually a simulated situation designed to duplicate laboratory conditions in the pupils' future job situations.

The *work-sample* approach places emphasis on both the product and the procedure, for with this approach pupils are required to perform some aspect of the total job which is being measured. This approach is used in an auto-mechanics class when a pupil is asked to repair a malfunctioning carburetor, to change spark plugs, or to work at some other specific task or tasks which give a representative work sample of the job of an automotive mechanic. The quality of the pupil's performance of the tasks then gives evidence of his likely success or failure in the job in question.

PLANNING PERFORMANCE TESTS

Performance tests have, as do other types of measurement, the requirement that considerable planning precede actual construction. In Chapter 2 the table of specifications for test construction was discussed and illustrated as an aid in constructing informal objective tests. Such an outline of specifications is also important in the construction of both performance and essay tests. In the planning of both kinds of tests, behavior objectives must also be stated, since desirable performance is constituted of specific kinds of desirable pupil behavior. The teacher in these performance areas should utilize subject content as a tool in directing pupils to achieve the skills, knowledges, and understandings that lead to behavior changes. Thus in the same manner as for an informal objective test, a table of specifications should be outlined from an enumeration of the content areas which have been taught and from a list of the behavior objectives which have been set as class goals.

A list of objectives for the industrial-arts field might include the following:

1. To equip pupils with the skills needed for home repairs and to stimulate them to make common repairs in their own homes.
2. To develop skillful use of the common hand and power tools.
3. To insure the observance of safety procedures in using these tools.
4. To interest pupils in the industrial-arts field through the construction of wood and metal projects.
5. To develop the skills and interests which will lead some pupils to the industrial-arts field as their vocational choice.

Content areas in the course might include:

1. Common hand tools and their use.
2. Common power tools and their use.
3. Qualities of various types of hard and soft wood.
4. Safety rules.
5. Joints: butt, miter, doweled, and mortise.
6. Fasteners: screws, nails, staples, corrugated fasteners, and glue.
7. Finishes: oil, wax, paint, varnish, shellac, lacquer, glass, and plastics.
8. Project selection and construction.

Figure 4.1 is an example of a table of specifications constructed from the objectives and content areas listed above. An examination of this table makes it immediately apparent that not all the objectives and content areas are adaptable to measurement by performance tests. The table does, however, give a general outline of the intended emphasis of measurement, and it also serves as a basis for the selection of measurement approaches and for the further planning underlying the instruments which are selected. The approaches

Behavior	Content Areas		
Objectives	1 2 3 4		5 6 7 8
1. *To equip pupils with the skills needed for home repairs and to stimulate them to make common repairs in their own homes*	Objective test		Work-sample test
2. *To develop skillful use of the common hand and power tools*	Objective test Identification test Rating scale		Work-sample test
3. *To insure the observance of safety procedures in using these tools*	Objective test Observation checklist		Work-sample test
4. *To interest pupils in the industrial-arts field through the construction of wood and metal projects*	Project construction (Rating scale)		
5. *To develop the skills and interests which will lead some pupils to the industrial-arts field as their vocational choice*	Interest checklist Essay examination Interview		

FIG. 4.1. *Table of Specifications for Measurement of Performance in Industrial Arts.*

selected in this instance and indicated on the table are: (1) objective tests to measure objectives 1, 2, 3, and the first four content areas; (2) an identification performance test to measure objective 2 and the second content area; (3) work-sample performance tests to measure objectives 1, 2, 3, and the last four content areas; (4) checklists and rating scales to aid in the measurement of several of the areas; and (5) an interview or possibly some essay questions to determine the extent of pupil interest—the concern of objective 5.

It is obvious that the complete measurement outlined in this table of specifications cannot be a one-shot measurement provided by a single test. Indeed, this table is an outline of the various measurements which the teacher will use during an entire term to get a balanced picture of how well each pupil learns the content and achieves those objectives which are emphasized throughout the whole period. There remains, then, only the problem of deciding when the tests will be given and planning and constructing appropriate instruments.

CONSTRUCTION OF PERFORMANCE TESTS

In order to give teachers a complete picture of how to proceed for complete performance measurement, methods of constructing the various instruments suggested in the table of specifications (Fig. 4.1) are discussed in this section. The task here is no more difficult than in conventional item-writing; but because many teachers are unfamiliar with the task, they are often uncertain about how to start. Although the table of specifications gives the general frame of reference for measurement, it is necessary as a second step to break down the procedure or product to be evaluated into specific topics which lend themselves to reliable measurement. In the example in Fig. 4.1 measurement of the first three objectives and the first four content areas can be partially accomplished with objective tests which will be constructed in the manner described in Chapter 3. The other performance instruments to be used for additional measurement are discussed below.

IDENTIFICATION TESTS

The identification approach emphasizes the product rather than the procedure, and this approach is most fruitful if the products to be identified represent an adequate sampling of significant aspects of the content area. In the example in Fig. 4.1 we are concerned with measuring the objective "to develop skillful use of the common hand and power tools" and the content area "common power tools and their use."

One identification exercise which might be useful here would relate to the parts and functions of the various machines which pupils use in the shop. Either the actual machines or pictorial representations of the machines could be used in the exercise. Use of the actual machines would lend authenticity to the test but would be less convenient and more time-consuming than use of a photograph or sketch. With a machine only one pupil at a time could work at the station identifying parts, whereas an illustration could be duplicated and handed out to the entire class so that all could work out the identification simultaneously.

Figure 4.2 is an example of the type of illustration that may be used in such a test. Each important part of the jointer in this sketch is numbered, and the numbered blanks provide sufficient space for the pupil to write in the name and indicate the function of the part to be identified.

This type of test can be scored in the same manner as matching tests, and some of the same rules should be observed in its construction. The following rules are most important in constructing identification tests.

1. *Adequate directions should be given so that pupils clearly understand the type of response called for.* If only identification is required, the method of identification should be explained; when both identification of parts and explanation of their function is required, the pupil should understand from the directions the dual nature of his task.

2. *When drawings are used, they should be carefully reproduced and clearly labeled.* On the other hand, if actual machines or products are used, the identification stations should be spaced far enough apart to discourage cheating and to facilitate necessary movement around the machines.

3. *Pupils should be asked to identify only significant parts of the product or drawing.* Asking pupils to identify unimportant parts reduces the value of a test because it encourages them to memorize the details for the sole purpose of doing well on the test. They will

DIRECTIONS: Below is a drawing of a jointer. Identify the numbered parts by placing the correct name and a brief description of the function for each part in the corresponding numbered blank at the bottom of the page.

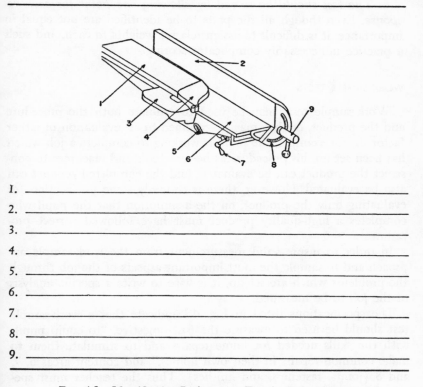

1. _____
2. _____
3. _____
4. _____
5. _____
6. _____
7. _____
8. _____
9. _____

FIG. 4.2. *Identification Performance Test for Industrial Arts.*

forget such information soon after they have taken the test unless there is continued motivation to retain it.

4. *Whenever feasible, pupils should be required to explain the function as well as to identify the item.* This improves the identification test by giving an indication of understanding in addition to measuring recall.

5. *The blanks for the responses should be uniform in length and should be conveniently arranged to facilitate scoring.* If the responses called for are of unequal length, the blanks should all be long enough to accommodate the longest response.

6. *The test should be scored by allowing one point for each response.* Even though all the parts to be identified are not equal in importance, it is difficult to assign relative weights to each, and such a practice unnecessarily complicates scoring.

WORK-SAMPLE TESTS

Work-sample tests may be used to evaluate both the procedure and the product, or they may be confined to an evaluation of either factor. If, for example, the pupil is working to complete a job which has been set up, his *procedure* as he uses tools and machines to construct the product can be evaluated, and the completed *product* can also be evaluated. However, there is certainly some justification for evaluating only the product, on the assumption that the pupil who completes a high-quality product must have followed correct procedures.

In order to insure valid measurement from the work-sample approach and to sample the most important aspects of the job through the problems which are set up, it is wise to write a specific analysis of the job to be measured.

The specifications listed in Fig. 4.1 indicate that a work-sample test should be used to measure the first objective, "to equip pupils with the skills needed for home repairs and to stimulate them to make common repairs in their own homes," and content areas 6, 7, and 8 (joints, fasteners, and finishes). Thus the teacher must specifically list and analyze the common home repairs and the skills required to make those repairs. When the analysis is complete, tasks can be set up to sample the most important elements in the list. These sample tasks can be set up in different areas of a room and numbered consecutively, so that pupils can proceed in an orderly manner from one task to another. Normally only one task is set up at each location. The setup is referred to as a *work-sample station*.

In setting up the work-sample stations, the teacher has the following alternatives: (1) he may use a minimum number of stations, each of which requires multiple skills, materials, and projects, or (2) he may use from 15 to 30 stations, each of which requires the use of one or two skills and/or materials. With the first alternative, each pupil might be asked to complete a specified project related to home repairs, following the specifications set up by the teacher. Such a project would include a specified type of joint, fastener, and finish so that each pupil's work could be compared to the written specification or to a model prepared by the teacher. Use of this approach would require several class periods to complete the evaluation, and both speed and quality would be considered in the scoring. A checklist would also be useful in objectifying the evaluation of the completed projects.

The work-station approach suggested in the second alternative provides a testing situation which can readily be completed in one class period. Here also it is necessary to confine the sample to significant and relevant tasks, skills, or identifications. When pupils are allowed approximately 1 minute at each station, from 15 to 30 stations can be included in a test designed to fit within the time limit of one class period.

EXAMPLES OF TYPICAL WORK-STATION PROBLEMS:
1. Identification of five samples of different types of wood finishes ordinarily used in homes.
2. Construction of a simple miter joint.
3. Location and drilling of two holes for countersunk screws at specified points on a board.
4. Identification of ten wood samples.

When stations are set up for performance-testing, the following suggestions for facilitating administration and scoring of the test should be followed:

1. The directions should indicate clearly both how the pupils are expected to respond and the sequence of the various stations.
2. The stations should be separated to prevent cheating.
3. The stations should be numbered, and all objects at each station should be lettered.
4. Time limits should be observed, with all pupils advancing from station to station when the signal to move is given.

5. All stations should be set up with independent problems which give no clue to the solution of problems at other stations.
6. To aid scoring, an answer sheet with written instructions and numbered and/or lettered spaces should be provided for the problem at each station.
7. Equal scoring weight should be allowed for each station.
8. A key providing all acceptable responses and procedures should be prepared as the stations are set up.

EVALUATION OF PERFORMANCE TESTS

CHECKLISTS

Checklists are particularly useful in evaluating procedures, and they are suggested as evaluation aids when the work-sample approach

---

DIRECTIONS: *As each pupil uses the circular saw, observe his procedure and place a check mark in the blank preceding each safety regulation with which he fails to comply.*

_____ 1. *He makes adjustments to the saw only when the power is turned off.*

_____ 2. *He uses the guard, kickback device, and spreader for all cuts except such special cuts as dadoes, etc.*

_____ 3. *He uses a pusher stick when ripping small pieces of stock.*

_____ 4. *He uses the ripping fence to guide the work when ripping stock.*

_____ 5. *He uses the crosscut gauge when crosscutting stock.*

_____ 6. *He never attempts to clear away scraps from the table top with his fingers while the saw is on.*

_____ 7. *He removes the ripping fence when crosscutting long pieces of stock.*

_____ 8. *He does not reach over and in back of the saw to pull pieces through.*

_____ 9. *He does not let tools and scrap stock pile up on the saw table.*

_____ 10. *He checks the stock before cutting to see that there are no nails, screws, or grit present in the wood.*

_____ 11. *He raises the saw blade no more than ⅛ inch above the stock being cut.*

_____ 12. *He asks the instructor to inspect special setups before beginning the cutting operation.*

FIG. 4.3. *Checklist for Evaluating Pupils' Compliance with Safety Regulations in Use of Circular Saw. (Adapted from Frank Paxton Lumber Co., Safety Rules for the Safe Operation of Power Woodworking Tools, Denver, Colo., pp. 8–9.)*

is used. Checklists are frequently used in industrial arts to help determine a pupil's adherence to safety procedures as he utilizes tools in project construction. An example of such a checklist is presented in Fig. 4.3.

A checklist is also useful in the simulated-conditions approach in a variety of other subject fields. For example, for evaluation in the field of chemistry, laboratory procedure could be broken down into a number of subdivisions, notably facility in handling laboratory equipment, observance of safety precautions, adherence to specified steps in experiments, and orderly and systematic recording of experimental steps and results. By further subdivision of these areas, a checklist or rating scale could be constructed to help objectify the instructor's evaluation of each pupil's laboratory procedure. The following example shows a checklist breakdown of one aspect of laboratory procedure.

DIRECTIONS: Check the items which characterize the pupil's laboratory procedure.

Facility in handling laboratory equipment.

_____ Uses appropriate equipment.
_____ Uses equipment efficiently and accurately.
_____ Sets up equipment quickly.
_____ Is careful with equipment.
_____ Has an orderly arrangement of required equipment.
_____ Recognizes inherent limitations of each item of equipment.
_____ Improvises or adapts equipment to the requirements of the experiment.

RATING SCALES

Although the checklists shown above and in Fig. 4.3 could readily be converted into rating scales for evaluating pupil performance, rating scales are discussed separately here to show their usefulness in product evaluation. Rating scales are constructed in the same manner as checklists, but they permit a numerical score to be given. Figure 4.4 is an example of a rating scale which can be used to evaluate woodworking projects. The scale is adapted for rating the finished product as well as the pupil's procedure as he constructs

DIRECTIONS: Rate each item in the scale on the basis of 4 points for outstanding quality or performance, 3 points for better than average, 2 points for average, 1 point for inferior, and 0 for unsatisfactory or failure. Encircle the appropriate number to indicate your rating, and enter the total of these numbers at the bottom of the sheet. If an item does not apply, draw a horizontal line through the item so that it will not be included in the total score.

Procedure Scale	
1. To what extent did he follow the detailed steps of his plan?	0 1 2 3 4
2. To what extent did he avoid having to do work over because of failure to follow his plan?	0 1 2 3 4
3. To what extent did he refrain from spoiling materials by working accurately and carefully?	0 1 2 3 4
4. To what extent did he follow approved procedures in performing specific operations?	0 1 2 3 4
5. To what extent did he exhibit skill in the use of:	
a. layout and measuring tools?	0 1 2 3 4
b. cutting edge tools?	0 1 2 3 4
c. boring and drilling tools?	0 1 2 3 4

Product Scale	
1. To what extent is the finished product an embodiment of the original plan?	0 1 2 3 4
2. Does the general appearance of the project reflect neat, orderly work?	0 1 2 3 4
3. Are the dimensions of the actual project the same as those on the drawing, within reasonable tolerances?	0 1 2 3 4
4. How do angular measurements check with those specified?	0 1 2 3 4
5. Of what quality is the finish?	0 1 2 3 4
6. To what extent were materials used to advantage?	0 1 2 3 4

6. To what extent did he show improvement in the use of tools? 0 1 2 3 4

7. Did he select the proper tool for each operation? 0 1 2 3 4

8. Did he use all tools properly? 0 1 2 3 4

9. To what extent did he exhibit initative in revising his plan as required by changing conditions? 0 1 2 3 4

10. Did he practice difficult operations to minimize material spoilage and poor workmanship? 0 1 2 3 4

11. To what extent did he keep profitably employed? Busy? 0 1 2 3 4

12. To what extent did he maintain a fair balance between quality of work performed and time consumed? 0 1 2 3 4

13. To what extent was he able to do his own work without assistance from instructor or other students? 0 1 2 3 4

7. Do all joints fit properly? 0 1 2 3 4

8. Are all margins uniform, curved and irregular lines properly executed, etc.? 0 1 2 3 4

FIG. 4.4. *Rating Scale for Projects in Industrial Arts.* (Adapted from *William J. Micheels and M. Ray Karnes, Measuring Educational Achievement, New York, McGraw-Hill, 1950, pp. 408–410.*)

the project. A similar scale could be designed for use in any class in which projects are constructed.

QUALITY SCALES

Quality scales are useful in determining the relative quality of such concrete products as handwriting, drawings, crafts projects, shop projects, and home economics projects. Quality scales are constructed by collecting examples of the product to be evaluated and selecting those eight or ten examples which most nearly approach uniform differences in quality. These examples will then represent a continuum from the best to the poorest, thus giving a scale against which each pupil's product can be evaluated.

In evaluating a product such as a garment, a shop project, or a painting, it is also sometimes desirable to use one of three ranking methods: (1) the method of paired comparisons, (2) the rank-order method, or (3) the equal-appearing interval method.

SUGGESTED READINGS

AHMANN, J. STANLEY, MARVIN D. GLOCK, and HELEN L. WARDEBERG, *Evaluating Elementary School Pupils,* Boston, Allyn and Bacon, 1960, 435 pp.
    The evaluation of products and procedures is discussed in Chapter 11. This chapter gives the teacher a good understanding of the problems involved in performance testing, but it lacks sufficient practical illustrations of test items.

BRADFIELD, JAMES M., and H. STEWART MOREDOCK, *Measurement and Evaluation in Education,* New York, Macmillan, 1957, 509 pp.
    This book includes in Chapter 5 and 13 a fine discussion of the evaluation of products and performance. Numerous helpful suggestions and practical illustrations of how to construct performance instruments are given.

MICHEELS, WILLIAM J., and M. RAY KARNES, *Measuring Educational Achievement,* New York, McGraw-Hill, 1950, 496 pp.
    Chapters 11, 12, 13, and 14 include a very thorough discussion of the various types of instruments for measuring performance, as well as helpful suggestions and practical illustrations for constructing these instruments.

WANDT, EDWIN, and GERALD W. BROWN, *Essentials of Educational Evaluation*, New York, Holt, 1957, 117 pp.

Chapter 4 has examples of rating scales and checklists which can be used in evaluating various types of pupil performance.

CHAPTER 5 *Construction and use of essay tests*

In many areas of learning there are situations in which specific, objective test problems cannot elicit the total information which a pupil possesses. Such problems may, in fact, serve to restrict and circumvent learning by focusing it only on those things which can be tested objectively. Creativity and original thinking are not best stimulated by alternate-choice questions; nor are the problems of living which pupils face or will face as adults so clear-cut as to present two well-defined alternatives. Rather, in either the creative situation or the life-problem situation there will be a number of possible avenues which must be explored, tried, and accepted or rejected. Freedom of response is an invaluable strength of the essay test, a strength which permits the pupil to enrich his answers with the countless facets of his experience and understanding, thus permitting the teacher a fuller insight into the total understanding which the pupil possesses.

Each type of test form discussed in this book has certain advantages not characteristic of other forms. Thus there is no best test form which teachers can use. Most fields and levels of teaching can be measured only with a balanced combination of test forms, each test form being selected to do the specific job for which it is best fitted.

USES OF ESSAY TESTS

Essay tests should be used to measure such objectives as understandings, attitudes, interests, creativity, and verbal expression. Teaching which stresses the Gestalt concepts of "wholeness" and insightful understanding of large concepts is most adaptable to essay examination, whereas the connectionist approach of presenting learning in smaller parts adapted to the learner is most compatible with objective techniques. Seldom, however, is a teaching approach wholly Gestalt or wholly connectionist; rather it is more frequently some combination of both, demanding the combined measurement approach.

Since the major strengths of the essay test are (1) the emphasis upon freedom of expression and creativity, and (2) the emphasis upon depth and scope of knowledge—upon the pupil's grasp of a total situation, it should be used in those fields most concerned with these objectives. It would be difficult to teach English and measure it effectively without using essay examinations as primary measurement instruments. Similarly some of the teaching objectives in the social sciences—history, government, sociology, and geography—are particularly adapted to essay measurement. The cause-and-effect relationship in an analysis of historical events certainly could not be adequately measured by objective instruments, although the use of essay measurement in these fields does not preclude the possibility of supplemental measurement through objective means.

PLANNING ESSAY TESTS

One of the common weaknesses in essay testing is the lack of teacher planning preceding the preparation of the test. It is not unusual for a teacher to wander casually into a classroom and write one broad, ambiguous question somewhat illegibly on the chalkboard—

in fact, the apparent lack of premeditation in such a procedure often leads pupils to speculate whether or not the question has been extemporaneously composed. In essay testing, planning is as important as in objective testing, although the planning is somewhat different in nature. Here, as in objective testing, the table of specifications, showing the teaching objectives and the content areas to be tested, is essential. Here also the decision to select the essay instrument must be based on the critical question: "Does the essay test best measure the objectives and content of the course?"

From this point on, however, the planning for the two types of tests takes deviate pathways. Planning for essay testing must take into account the limited nature of the test sample, the time limits of the class period, and the choice of material which is adaptable to a test sample. Furthermore, this planning must include consideration of the bases which will be used for grading the answers. A decision must be made on whether to include a limited number of extended-response questions, a variety of restricted-response questions, or a balanced combination of the two types—a decision again based upon the content and objectives to be measured.

The major problems to be considered in the planning stage are: (1) Are the material and objectives to be measured adaptable to an essay test? (2) Do the pupils have sufficient background, both in composition and in the subject area, to write an essay test? (3) Does the test permit freedom of response sufficient to permit the pupils to bring to bear the depth and scope of their knowledge, or is it so restricted that the objective test could elicit the same type of response? (4) Has sufficient time been allotted the pupils to plan their responses so that they are more than mere disjointed associations of somewhat relevant statements?

CONSTRUCTION OF ESSAY TESTS

The actual writing of essay-test questions would require little time were it not for the fact that the answers to the questions and the grading criteria should also be prepared at the time the questions are written. The lack of clear-cut, carefully planned answers written out by the teacher before the test is administered is one of the main reasons why essay tests are graded so unreliably. The following suggestions will help the teacher construct better essay tests and get better results from them.

1. *The questions should be written with care, and the language selected should be precise in meaning and unambiguous.* The area covered by a question should be carefully defined and restricted so that pupils are required to write to the point and may not "shoot the bull" or muddle the issue by including extraneous material in their responses.

2. *Time and thought should be given to the actual selection and preparation of the questions.* The limited number of questions which can be included in an essay test makes selection extremely important, and only those questions which measure important objectives and content should be included.

3. *The directions for the test should be explicitly written out.* These directions should included mention of the relative grade value of each question and should indicate if such factors as organization, grammar, spelling, and handwriting are to be considered in the grading. The following example includes the important information which should be included in the directions of an essay examination:

DIRECTIONS: Each of the following four questions has a value of 20 points. Spend approximately the same amount of writing time on each question. Since the organization of your answers will be a factor in your grade, you should spend the first few minutes outlining your answers before you begin to write.

4. *There should be no optional questions on the test.* When the pupil is permitted to choose from among several questions on the test, he may avoid some questions which measure important objectives. Although question options do help the test psychology of pupils, they complicate an already difficult grading problem by making it virtually impossible to get comparable scores.

5. *Open-book essay tests should be avoided.* Although such examinations may help the pupil who fears tests, most studies have shown that the reliability of a test is little affected by permitting pupils to

use the book during the examination. The best pupils still tend to get the high grades and the poor pupils to get the low grades. In fact, if anything, the good pupil gains some advantage because, through familiarity with the text and superior reading skill, he can locate quickly any points which he needs; whereas the poor pupil reads slowly and lacks the study skills which would permit him to locate the answers speedily. If the measurement objective is one of familiarizing pupils with the learning material, it can be argued that open-book tests are useful. On the other hand, granting that some learning might take place, it is obvious that it is short-term learning, quickly forgotten, and that there are more effective teaching techniques for familiarizing pupils with the learning material.

6. *Pupils should be given advance notice of essay tests.* When pupils are given advance notice of an essay test, they are motivated to study effectively. Also, when pupils know that the test will be of the essay type, they may use study techniques, such as outlining, which improve the long-term retention of the information learned. It is important, incidentally, to give advance notice for *all* types of examinations, with the possible exception of short quizzes, to insure effective review.

7. *Pupils should be given training in taking essay tests.* Pupils who have taken only objective tests during their school careers frequently do not know how to write essay tests, and they may be so frightened of the tests that they perform much below their optimum levels. It is helpful to give pupils periodic practice on several short essay questions which have little or no grade value, in order to provide a permissive atmosphere in which they can perform at their best level. Also, informing pupils that test time should be taken to plan the answers before they begin to write and instructing them in preparing outlines for their answers will pay dividends in the quality of response.

8. *Validity of the essay test is improved by restricting its use to the measurement of content and objectives to which this test form is best adapted.* For example, if the content to be measured consists mostly of factual data, then use objective means of measurement, which are much more reliable.

9. *The reliability and the extent of the sample for essay tests can be improved by increasing the number of questions and varying the types of questions.* A combination of extended-response and restricted-response questions permits more questions to be included in the test and makes it possible to measure a greater number of teaching objectives. It is also true that many restricted-response questions can be graded much more reliably than can the extended-response type. Some restricted-response questions, such as the outline question, can be graded as reliably as objective questions.

TYPES OF ESSAY TESTS

There are many types of essay tests, although teachers tend to limit themselves to the use of the broad discussion type. Essay questions can be roughly classified into the two categories of *extended-response* and *restricted-response* items. The extended-response question is one which is relatively unstructured, permitting the pupil freedom in organizing and expressing the answer in a manner that displays his personal insights and the breadth and scope of his knowledge. Discussion questions fall into this extended-response classification, e.g., "Discuss the tax structure of the local, state, and federal branches of government in the United States."

The restricted-response question is much more easily graded than the extended-response type, for the pupils' answers are closely circumscribed. The definition question is a good example of such a question, e.g., "Define the term *catalyst*." Restricted-response items are sometimes called short-essay items, and the instructions to the pupil may be quite specific. The following is an example of a question which specifically restricts the response.

Discuss three techniques of instruction—lecture, demonstration, and class discussion. List the principles which should be followed in using each technique. What subjects are best adapted to each technique?

This example of the restricted response, rather than limiting the length of the response, restricts the area within which the pupil may write.

The variety of possible types of essay questions and examples of each type are shown in Monroe and Carter's list.[1]

1. *Selective recall—basis given.*
   Name the presidents of the United States who had been in military life before their election.
   What do New Zealand and Australia sell in Europe that may interfere with our market?

2. *Evaluating recall—basis given.*
   Which do you consider the three most important American inventions in the nineteenth century from the standpoint of expansion and growth of transportation?
   Name the three statesmen who have had the greatest influence on economic legislation in the United States.

3. *Comparison of two things—on a single designated basis.*
   Compare Eliot and Thackeray in ability in character delineation.
   Compare the armies of the North and South in the Civil War as to leadership.

4. *Comparison of two things—in general.*
   Compare the early settlers of the Massachusetts colony with those of the Virginia colony.
   Contrast the life of Silas Marner in Raveloe with his life in Lantern Yard.

5. *Decision—for or against.*
   Whom do you admire more, Washington or Lincoln?
   In which, in your opinion, can you do better, oral or written examinations?

6. *Causes or effects.*
   Why has the Senate become a much more powerful body than the House of Representatives?
   What caused Silas Marner to change from what he was in Lantern Yard to what he was in Raveloe?

7. *Explanation of the use of exact meaning of some phrase or statement in a passage.*
   Tell how a siphon works.
   What did Hamlet mean by "be" when he said "To be or not to be, that is the question"?

[1] Walter S. Monroe and R. E. Carter, "The Use of Different Types of Thought Questions in Secondary Schools and Their Relative Difficulty for Students," *Bureau of Educational Research Bulletin,* No. 14, Urbana, University of Illinois, 1923.

8. *Summary of some unit of the text or of some article read.*
State the plot of *The House of Seven Gables* in about one hundred words.
Tell briefly the contents of the Declaration of Independence.

9. *Analysis. (The word itself is seldom involved in the question.)*
What characteristic of Silas Marner makes you understand why Raveloe people were suspicious of him?
Mention several qualities of leadership.

10. *Statement of relationship.*
Why is a knowledge of botany helpful in studying agriculture?
Tell the relation of exercise to good health.

11. *Illustration of examples (your own) or principles of science, construction in language, etc.*
Give two examples of the use of pure carbon in industrial work.
Illustrate the *incorrect* use of a relative pronoun with a parenthetical phrase.

12. *Classification. (Usually the converse of number 11.)*
Group the following words according to their parts of speech and name each group: red, boy, run, house, in, with, small, slowly, ball, etc.
What do four of the five men named below have in common?
Aristotle, Pericles, Homer, Cicero, Phidias.

13. *Application of rules or principles in these situations.*
Would you weigh more or less on the moon? On the sun? Why?
If you sat halfway between the middle and one end of a seesaw, would a person sitting on the other end have to be heavier or lighter than you in order to make the seesaw balance in the middle? Why?

14. *Discussion.*
Discuss the Monroe Doctrine.
Discuss early American literature.

15. *Statement of aim—author's purpose in his selection or organization of material.*
What was the purpose of introducing this incident?
Why did he discuss [this] before [that]?

16. *Criticism—as to the adequacy, correctness, or relevancy of a printed statement or a classmate's answer to a question on the lesson.*
Why were the Articles of Confederation doomed to failure?
What is wrong with the following menu? (*Menu given below.*)

17. *Outline.*

Outline the foreign policy of the Federal government during the Civil War.

Outline the steps required in computing the square root of a five-figure number.

18. *Reorganization of facts.* (*A good type of review question to give training in organization.*)

The student is asked for reports where facts from different organizations are arranged on an entirely new basis.

19. *Formulation of new questions—problems and questions raised.*

What question came to your mind?

What else must be known in order to understand the matter under consideration?

20. *New methods of procedure.*

Suggest a plan for proving the truth or falsity of some hypothesis.

How would you change the plot in order to produce a certain different effect?

In addition to the above types, restricted-response questions which require pupils to recall a list of rules, facts, or specific information, as well as the definition-type question referred to earlier, are often classified as essay-type. It is obvious, then, that the imaginative teacher who wishes to use essay-testing has at his command a variety of question types adaptable to many types of objectives.

GRADING ESSAY TESTS

The most time-consuming aspect of using an essay test is the grading; however, careful attention to planning and construction of the instrument yields results at this later stage. If, during the process of constructing the test, the teacher has set up the grading standards and prepared an answer key, grades can be assigned rather easily. Yet with extended-response questions even a carefully prepared key may leave out some important points which one or two of the pupils include in their answers; the teacher should determine beforehand whether he will permit extra credit for these points or whether he will add the points to the grading key and use them as a basis for grading all papers.

METHODS OF GRADING

There are two acceptable methods for grading essay tests: (1) the point-score method and (2) the sorting method. With either method it is important that the papers be graded without identifying the pupil and that all of the papers be graded at one sitting. Grading the papers without looking at the names of the pupils or attempting to identify them helps the reader to avoid the "halo effect" which frequently plagues essay readers. Grading all of the papers during one work session lessens the possibility of changing the grading standards from one group of papers to another. It is possible, however, that fatigue might be a factor which would make it mandatory to read the papers in several groups when there are a great many papers to be graded. In such cases a conscious effort should be made to adhere to the same grading standards and to use the same criteria for all papers.

Of the two methods for grading essay tests, the point-score method seems more defensible, although it is time-consuming and requires more handling of the papers than does the sorting method. The procedure for grading by the point-score method consists of three steps:

1. Construct a grading key which includes the major aspects which the pupil should include in his response to each question. Assign a total point value to each question along with the relative point value for each aspect of the response.
2. Read a single question through all the papers, assigning the appropriate number of points to the response on each paper as it is read. Repeat the procedure until all questions on all of the papers have been read. It is important that pupils not be identified so that the only criterion for judgment is the thoroughness with which each pupil covered all aspects of the question.
3. Total the points on each paper after all of the questions have been read; then assign a letter grade to each paper on the basis of established norms, percentages, or a curve.

The two major advantages of this procedure in grading are: (1) it gives a grade which is defensible because it is based upon a carefully prepared key, and a point-score total for each pupil can be arrived at from a comparison of his answers to that key, and (2) it permits the reader to grade each question through all of the papers without changing his mind-set, as would be necessary if he were to read all of the questions on each pupil's paper before proceeding to the next paper. This method also makes it possible for the reader to grade the papers in several sessions rather than in one long continuous session, thus reducing the fatigue problem and the possibility of changing grading standards. With this method it is permissible to take a break in reading when a single question has been read since any change in standard, toward either leniency or strictness, which the grader may unconsciously make after the break, will affect all the papers equally—but on subsequent questions only.

The sorting method for grading essays is simpler than the point-score method, but it is an effective method which insures very good results if it is carefully followed. This method includes the following essential steps:

1. Read through all the papers as quickly as possible, sorting them as they are read into a predetermined number of piles which represent the different letter grades to be assigned to the papers. During this first reading those papers which do not clearly fall into any one pile should be identified with question marks and put into the pile which seems closest to the grade of the paper. For example, if after having read a paper, the reader is in doubt as to whether the paper merits a C or a B grade but decides that it seems closer to a B, he will place a question mark on the paper and put it in the B pile.

2. Reread the papers, giving special attention to those which carry a question mark. In the instances when change is warranted during this rereading, papers may be changed from one pile to another. Those who use this method sometimes do not read all of the papers a second time, confining their second reading to those papers which have been marked as questionable. All of the papers should be reread, however, especially if the first reading is a cursory one.

3. Assign letter grades on the basis of the piles into which the papers were sorted.

Although there are arguments in favor of both methods, the point-score method would appear to be the more advantageous in that it seems to improve the reliability of the essay grade. In the interests of time economy, however, there may be reason to select the sorting method, which gives reasonable reliability if it is carefully used.

PROBLEMS OF GRADING

There are several special problems in grading essay examinations, regardless of the method used. Four of these problems deserve special attention: (1) the halo effect, (2) high-grading or generosity error, (3) low-grading or penalty error, and (4) the influence of extraneous factors.

The *halo effect* is encountered both in rating scales and in essay tests. The halo effect is apparent when the grader reads a paper in which the first question is well organized and answered extremely well but is followed by answers to several other questions which are not particularly well done. In spite of the poorer performance in the latter answers the paper is assigned a high score because of the halo carry-over from the first answer. Familiarity with a pupil's work may have the same effect if the pupil's paper is identified during reading. If a good pupil's paper is being read, his past high performance may influence the reader to assign too high a grade when the performance on a particular paper is actually poor. The *reverse halo effect* also has to be guarded against. The poor pupil is often graded too low when he writes a good paper; and a poor first answer on a test may influence the reader to lower the grade on subsequent questions.

Generosity error is related to the halo effect. The grader who is affected by generosity error consistently assigns grades which are too high to all of the papers. He may give half or more of the class A and B grades even when class performance justifies an approximation of the normal curve in grade distribution. It is well, in fact, for the teacher to look periodically at his grade distributions to see how closely they approximate the normal distribution curve. Deviations from the curve are certainly justifiable when the intellectual caliber of a class is definitely high or low.

The *penalty error* which is imposed on a class by a strict grader is as unfair as the generosity error, and it also arises from a distorted concept of pupil achievement. Some teachers consistently hold standards which are too high for their classes to achieve. Challenging standards of achievement are worthwhile when the challenge is one which the class is capable of accepting. If, however, the challenge is too high, frustration will inevitably result. Teachers whose distribution of class grades is consistently low should re-examine their standards, the quality of their teaching, and IQ level of the class, for it is not always the pupils who are at fault.

The problem of *extraneous factors* influencing the grading of essay tests is one which is extremely difficult to overcome, although a teacher who is cognizant of this influence may compensate for it to some degree. The quality of handwriting is a factor which often introduces a detrimental bias into a pupil's grade. If the paper is difficult to read, the pupil may be unjustly penalized. Other factors are grammar, spelling, organization, vocabulary, neatness, and composition ability. All of these factors may legitimately be considered and given weight in grading, but only when they are part of the teaching and measurement objectives and when the pupils have been informed that the factors are to be given grade weight.

SUGGESTED READINGS

AHMANN, J. STANLEY, MARVIN D. GLOCK, and HELEN L. WARDEBERG, *Evaluating Elementary School Pupils*, Boston, Allyn and Bacon, 1960, 435 pp.
  Chapter 9 gives suggestions for improving the essay test as well as methods of grading which improve reliability.
GERBERICH, J. RAYMOND, HARRY A. GREENE, and ALBERT N. JORGENSEN, *Measurement and Evaluation in the Modern School*, New York, McKay, 1962, 622 pp.

All of Part 3 in this text deals with test construction, but Chapter 9 gives specific consideration to oral and essay tests.

WOOD, DOROTHY ADKINS, *Test Construction*, Columbus, Ohio, Merrill, 1960, 134 pp.

Chapter 10 includes a brief discussion of the essay test and gives some suggestions for improving its use.

WRIGHTSTONE, J. WAYNE, JOSEPH JUSTMAN, and IRVING ROBBINS, *Evaluation in Modern Education*, New York, American Book, 1956, 481 pp.

Chapter 6 includes discussion of both essay and oral tests.

CHAPTER 6 *Construction and use of oral examinations*

The oral examination is the oldest form of examination used by teachers. Early teachers relied wholly on this form, and the Greek philosopher-teacher, Socrates, has often been cited as a model for emulation in the use of the oral-questioning technique. The oral examination also has a time-honored place at the graduate level of education. the oral thesis examination has been used continuously at the master's and doctoral levels since its introduction at the University of Paris in 1215 A.D. Oral examinations were used almost exclusively in this country until a little over a century ago, when Horace Mann introduced written essay examinations in the Boston elementary schools. The relatively recent development and refinement of other test forms, notably objective types, has influenced most teachers to relegate oral examinations to the status of a teaching technique. The modern teacher rarely attempts to grade every oral contribution of his pupils; however, there are still some teachers who utilize the oral quiz to assess both the achievement of their pupils and the effectiveness of the previous day's presentation. Certainly the oral examination is not without merit as a measurement device, although it has frequently been misapplied by teachers inexperienced in its use. When properly constructed and used, it can be both a good instructional technique and a valuable, informal means of appraising pupil progress.

TYPES OF ORAL EXAMINATIONS

Unfortunately, when the oral examination is mentioned, the typical teacher conjures up a picture of a classroom situation in which the teacher spends a class period asking each pupil in turn one question and then enters a grade for each in his grade book. Obviously such a practice has little measurement value, although it must be admitted that it probably stimulates pupils to do some daily studying and may thus be a useful teaching device. The oral examination as it is discussed in this chapter, however, does not have such a limited definition as that illustrated in the above situation. There are numerous types of oral examinations which have a variety of uses in measurement and teaching; and although there is enough similarity among most of the types to permit them to be discussed as a group, some types of oral examinations are highly specialized and must necessarily be considered separately. For convenience of discussion the following classification of oral examinations is suggested:

1. Orally administered examinations which require an oral response. Actually these examinations can be grouped into two types: (1) those in which single questions are asked individuals in a group situation, and (2) those in which numerous questions are posed to a single individual. The classroom situation described previously, in which each pupil in turn is asked a question, is an example of the first type; the oral thesis examination given to graduate students is an example of the second type.
2. Orally administered examinations which require a written response. These may include teacher-constructed tests, auditory comprehension examinations, or tests for nonreaders, such as the readiness tests given to preschool or first-grade pupils.

3. Orally administered examinations of the standardized type. These include some of the best intelligence tests, such as the Wechsler, and many of the projective personality tests, such as the Rorschach. In addition, hearing tests may require both oral administration and oral response.

4. Interviews in which persons are selected for particular responsibilities or positions. Most good jobs require that the competing applicants be interviewed.

PLANNING ORAL EXAMINATIONS

Much of the misuse of the oral examination is probably due to poor planning. As with other forms of tests, success in measurement with an oral examination is proportional to the care which has been exercised in planning it. Obviously little worthwhile measurement will result from any test which is hurriedly and haphazardly concocted. In preparing oral examinations, care should be taken with the following planning steps.

First, the objectives and content areas should be listed to form a test outline or table of specifications similar to that suggested for the informal objective test. With oral examinations this outline need not be so elaborate as that for objective tests, since the test will probably be used to measure only a limited number of objectives and content areas. Also these objectives are likely to be quite explicit, and probably only one or two large content areas will be included although the area or areas will be broken down into specifics.

Second, the type of oral examination should be selected on the basis of the table of specifications. The teacher should keep in mind that oral questions are particularly well adapted to an extended pupil response such as that required in essay examinations, but an extended response can be given much more quickly orally than in writing, and the response does not have to be read in order to be graded. On the other hand, specific facts can be readily measured by a written objective examination, and the oral examination should not be heavily weighted with such items.

CONSTRUCTION OF ORAL EXAMINATIONS

Although the construction of several of the oral forms is not difficult, it is apparent that some time must be spent in preparing the questions if the desired measurement is to be accomplished. Perhaps the two most important principles to be observed in constructing the oral examination are: (1) the questions should be written out ahead of time, and (2) acceptable answers should be written for each of the questions constructed. Also, although it varies with the type and purpose of examination, the method of grading should be decided upon before the test is constructed, and relative grade weights should be assigned to the items as they are written. This preplanning, along with care in writing the items, will insure the teacher against the common and frequently justified criticism that oral examinations have little use in measurement.

ORAL QUESTIONS—ORAL RESPONSES

Oral questions which require oral responses should be similar to questions written for an essay examination. They can be either restricted-response or extended-response questions, but it must be kept in mind that not many questions calling for an extended response can be given within the time limits of a regular class period. The type and number of questions are also determined by whether the pupils are to be tested individually or as a group. Individual testing permits a teacher to ask each pupil a number of questions; and since 10 to 15 minutes may be devoted to testing each pupil, some of the questions can require an extended response, although the majority should be the restricted-response type. When a group of pupils is tested, probably all of the questions should be of the restricted-response type, since about 35 to 40 questions will be prepared if each pupil is to answer at least one question. Also, with the normal class period of 45 to 55 minutes, in group testing about one minute can be allotted for the answer to each question.

The following five questions are oral restricted-response questions. They are designed to help an American history teacher determine from the oral group situation how effectively he has taught the topic, "The Post-Civil War Reconstruction Period."

1. Mention three significant reasons why the Southerners became Democrats.
2. What constitutional amendment gave Negroes the right to vote?
3. What was President Johnson's attitude toward the defeated South?
4. What were the chief agricultural products of the South during the post-Civil War period?
5. What proportion of the southern population was white and what proportion was Negro?

These questions stress recall and, with the exception of the third question, can be answered in one sentence. About 30 such questions would certainly give an adequate review of the topic and should give the teacher a good indication of whether or not the class has sufficiently mastered the subject matter to proceed to the next topic.

The five questions given above would also be appropriate if each pupil were examined individually. However, in the individual examination several extended-response questions similar to the following question could also be included in order to give the teacher an opportunity to observe how well the pupil expresses himself and how quickly and logically he thinks.

How could the long, difficult reconstruction period have been avoided or alleviated so that there would not have been the bitter antagonism which plagued North-South political relationships for the rest of the century?

Even though such a question is difficult and probably will be incompletely answered by the pupil, some of the alternative solutions to the problem will previously have been discussed in class so that he will have an opportunity to exercise his critical judgment in responding to the question.

In working with primary grade pupils who have not yet learned to write or read well, oral examinations requiring an oral response are essential. Even with the more advanced pupils who can take short written tests, orally administered written examinations are useful.

In the upper grades retarded readers may also perform better on oral than on written examinations because their reading handicap is generally accompanied by inability to express themselves well in writing, and they are generally afraid of written tests because of their previous poor performances on them.

ORAL QUESTIONS—WRITTEN RESPONSES

The same types of restricted-response and extended-response questions suggested earlier for the oral-response examination can be administered orally when pupils are required to give written responses. Fewer questions should be included in this examination, however, since pupils obviously write more slowly than they speak. There are several instances when this form of examination may be used instead of the examination which is entirely written. There is some justification for the orally administered examination when there is inadequate time to duplicate the test, a shortage of supplies and clerical help, or too few duplicating machines.

Occasionally, too, a teacher may be interested in getting some indication of the level of auditory comprehension of his pupils, which would again justify oral administration of a written examination. Since much of the instruction in schools depends upon oral communication with such teaching techniques as lectures, class discussions, and oral reports, it may well be true that not enough stress is placed on the measurement of auditory comprehension. In measuring auditory comprehension, however, it is undoubtedly better to use objective-type questions rather than the essay type discussed above. It is also extremely important that the teacher who administers such an examination read well and that he speak loudly and slowly and enunciate clearly to enable those who are listening to respond correctly if they know the answers.

In several secondary school subject areas there is major stress on auditory comprehension. This is true of foreign language conversation classes and of shorthand. Conversation in a foreign language which requires a verbal response as well as auditory comprehension is discussed later in the section on oral performance examinations.

Shorthand, on the other hand, requires a written response from verbal stimuli. In a sense shorthand teachers are particularly fortunate since they need not, as do many teachers, rely upon the types of measurement which are poorly correlated with desired performance. In shorthand the job-performance situation can be closely simulated in the classroom dictation period; thus both measurement and teaching are readily related to the desired job performance, and those who perform well in the class usually perform equally well in business positions.

ORAL PERFORMANCE EXAMINATIONS

The oral performance examination is particularly well adapted to such areas as speech, dramatics, and foreign language. Both speech and dramatics stress verbal performance, and the quality of the performance cannot be measured by a written examination. In fact, the measurement of performance is largely subjective as judged by the teacher and the observers. As an aid in directing the attention of the evaluators to the specific aspects of the performance which are most important, it is useful to construct a checklist or rating scale which is based on an analysis of the desirable elements involved in a good performance. For example, some of the desirable elements in a good speaking performance are: (1) logical organization, (2) correct grammar, (3) good word choice, (4) appropriate gestures, (5) good stage presence, and (6) audience rapport. An example of an evaluation sheet useful in evaluating the performance of a speaker is shown in Fig. 6.1.

Dramatic performances can be evaluated in much the same manner as speaking performances; and since the success of these performances is often directly related to the response which they stimulate in an audience, it is good practice for a teacher to let his pupils help evaluate the performance by filling out evaluation sheets.

Foreign language performance tests should be different from those in speech and dramatics because the teaching objectives are concerned with both written and reading performance in addition to verbal performance. Some foreign language courses, however, primarily stress oral performance or conversation; and the conversational approach, including auditory comprehension, is becoming increasingly important in modern foreign language instruction. In such courses the daily conversation periods with the class have both instructional and measurement functions. These periods should be planned in such a way as to provide sufficient opportunity for each

---

DIRECTIONS: *Evaluate the speaker by circling the number which most nearly represents his performance on each of the specific aspects listed below. For superior performance circle 4, above-average performance 3, average performance 2, below-average performance 1, and unsatisfactory performance 0.*

Item	Rating
1. Rapport with audience	4 3 2 1 0
2. Enthusiastic, interesting presentation	4 3 2 1 0
3. Effective organization of material	4 3 2 1 0
4. Clarity of presentation	4 3 2 1 0
5. Correct grammar usage	4 3 2 1 0
6. Good word choice	4 3 2 1 0
7. Adequate knowledge of subject	4 3 2 1 0
8. Significance of material presented	4 3 2 1 0
9. Good stage presence	4 3 2 1 0
10. Appropriate gestures	4 3 2 1 0
Total effectiveness of presentation	

FIG. 6.1. *Scale for Evaluating a Speaking Performance.*

pupil to participate so that the teacher obtains an adequate sample of each pupil's performance over a period of several weeks. Rather than give the conventional letter grade for daily performances, some teachers have found it convenient to use a three-symbol scale consisting of +/ for superior performance, / for average performance, and -/ for below-average performance. These symbols are then averaged at the end of the grading period and translated into a letter grade to be weighed as one factor in the nine-week or semester grade.

PRINCIPLES OF USE

Several of the principles which should be followed in using the oral examination have been referred to earlier in the sections on planning and constructing the examination, but they are important enough to be reviewed at this point.

1. *Skillful administration of the oral examination is necessary to achieve good measurement.* The pupil must hear and understand the questions if he is to respond to them successfully; therefore the teacher should *read the questions loudly and slowly and enunciate carefully.* When the examination is administered to pupils individually, the teacher should have a friendly but businesslike attitude to help establish a desirable rapport with the pupil. Time limits should also be observed, and an effort should be made to keep the conditions of individual examination relatively standard if the results are to be compared.

2. *The type of oral examination used should be adaptable to the field in which it is used.* As noted previously, there are several types of oral examinations which are useful for a variety of measurement purposes. However, there are some fields for which the oral examination is not adaptable as a measuring device, although it may have some teaching value. Examples of excellent adaptation of oral examinations to subject fields are the oral performance examination for speech and drama and the auditory-comprehension examination for foreign language and shorthand.

3. *When the oral examination is used primarily for teaching or review purposes, little or no grading weight should be given to the examination.* Oral examinations used for these purposes are excellent tools to stimulate study, to review topics previously taught, and to give a teacher a good idea of how well his group has grasped the concepts, ideas, and facts which had been taught in the preceding day's lesson. The following procedure has been found useful in this particular adaptation of the oral examination:

1. Fifteen to thirty questions which give a review of the topics to be tested are constructed.

2. Each pupil is asked to number his test sheet from 1 to 30.
3. The questions are then asked of different individuals in the class, but each pupil is asked to keep a record of the questions he could answer, indicating on his sheet by "yes" or "no" whether he could answer the questions.
4. At the end of the questioning period pupils are asked to count the number of questions which they could have answered. The results are then summarized on the chalkboard through a poll to determine the number who got all the questions correct, the number who missed one question, etc., until the bottom score is reached.

This procedure gives a frequency table that the teacher can examine to determine class success and that individual pupils can examine to determine their relative standing in the class. When pupils are notified of such an examination ahead of time, they will study for it; and if they know that their grades will not be recorded, they are willing to keep honest, accurate records of their individual performance.

4. When only one question is asked each pupil, *care must be taken to keep all questions comparable in difficulty* or at least to adjust the difficulty of the question to the competence of the pupil. Oral quizzes in which only one question is asked each pupil obviously lack reliability because the sample is inadequate; reliability is often further reduced by capricious variation in question difficulty.

5. Although grading of oral exams is usually subjective, *an effort should be made to eliminate the influence of extraneous factors such as favoritism.* The use of checklists and rating scales whenever possible will increase the objectivity of grading, and prewritten answers also give a criterion for judging the comprehensiveness of the pupils' answers.

SPECIAL ADVANTAGES OF ORAL EXAMINATIONS

In special situations and special fields, oral examinations have the following advantages over other test forms:
1. Oral questioning permits the examiner to be flexible in his

procedure. He may adapt his questions to fit a pupil's individual background, or he may elicit additional meanings behind vague or incomplete statements by posing new questions during the course of an examination. This flexibility is desirable in individual intelligence tests and in oral examinations for candidates for graduate degrees.

2. Oral examination of an individual pupil is an excellent means of following the thought processes which he has used in solving problems, particularly in such fields as mathematics. Used for this purpose, the oral examination may become a valuable tool for the diagnosis of pupil difficulties.

3. Skillful questioning by the teacher may also help the pupil apply information which he possesses to the solution of new problems or to see implications in related situations which he had not heretofore recognized.

4. Oral examinations are more valid than other test forms for measuring subjects in which verbal performance is stressed.

5. Less time is needed to prepare most oral examinations than is required for other types of tests, although the need for careful planning and construction is the same for all types.

SUGGESTED READINGS

There are few references which give separate consideration to the oral examination; however, the following references contain discussion of both oral and essay examinations.

GERBERICH, J. RAYMOND, HARRY A. GREENE, and ALBERT N. JORGENSEN, *Measurement and Evaluation in the Modern School*, New York, McKay, 1962, 622 pp. (Chapter 9).

WRITHSTONE, J. WAYNE, JOSEPH JUSTMAN, and IRVING ROBBINS, *Evaluation in Modern Education*, New York, American Book, 1956, 481 pp. (Chapter 6).

CHAPTER 7 *Characteristics*
of good measuring instruments

Good measuring results from careful planning, construction, and administration of tests, but the value of measurement is lost if the process stops at this point. Educational measurement instruments are made for the purpose of determining the extent of pupil achievement. If the achievement is satisfactory, the instruction must have been satisfactory. However, in order to determine whether the achievement can be deemed satisfactory, the teacher must first diagnose and evaluate the results of measurement. Frequently this evaluation leads to replanning and redirection of the instructional program in order to emphasize the learning areas in which pupils have shown marked weakness. It is thus through a close working relationship between teaching and measurement that the most effective instruction is attained.

All measuring instruments possess to some degree three important qualities: (1) validity, (2) reliability, and (3) usability. Of course, other qualities are important, but these three are the essentials without which a testing instrument would be useless. A brief example will serve to illustrate these qualities. In building a house, a carpenter uses several measuring instruments, and his choice of instruments depends upon the specific task at which he is working. If he wishes to lay out the foundation, he will select a steel tape; if he wishes to measure and fit a window, he will select a square. Both of these instruments are valid for measuring dimensions, but the steel tape is more useful and has greater reliability and accuracy than the square for measuring the gross dimensions of the house. On the other hand, the square with its finer dimensions is more useful and reliable for measuring the smaller areas.

The term *validity* refers to an instrument's truthfulness, *reliability* to its consistency, and *usability* to its practicality. In this chapter we are concerned with these characteristics as they apply to various teacher-made tests.

VALIDITY

Of the three qualities mentioned above, validity is the most important. A valid instrument is truthful because it measures what the person using the instrument wishes or attempts to measure. Obviously any instrument which does not perform this function is worthless; and the degree to which it does perform the function satisfactorily, called its relative validity, determines its degree of usefulness.

Furthermore, validity is specific, since an instrument has validity only for the purpose for which it was intended. This can be illustrated by the fact that an English grammar test which has high validity for measuring English grammar probably has virtually no validity for measuring algebra.

DETERMINATION OF VALIDITY

There have generally been two approaches to the determination of the relative validity of achievement tests: (1) the curricular approach and (2) the statistical approach. In the curricular approach, which is actually a rational approach, it is assumed that the curriculum in the specific field as represented by textbooks, courses of study, and expert opinion is valid; and the test content is compared against these criteria to determine its validity. For a more specific determination of curricular validity, a teacher, as the expert, examines his course outline and his teaching objectives to determine the degree to which they coincide with test content.

Because it is reasonable to assume that local educational needs, hence educational objectives and curricula, will show some variation, the consequent difference in educational emphasis makes it impossible to devise a standardized test which will have equal validity in all localities. Thus the teacher who constructs his tests to fit his individual objective can expect higher validity from these tests than from standardized tests which merely approximate his objectives and content; but he should begin to look critically on his objectives if the deviation becomes too great. Twentieth-century improvements in transportation and communication have permitted a degree of cultural interplay and regional idea-sharing which makes a common, good environment for all people much nearer realization than was ever before possible in any country. In this light, local differences are no longer as marked as they once were, and local educational variations are less necessary. In fact, those who travel from state to state visiting schools are often struck by the fact that our 50 state school systems are so much alike that in most cases only the geographic scenery shows much difference.

When the statistical approach is used to validate a test, a criterion which is presumed to have validity is selected, and the test scores of a group of examinees are correlated with that criterion. Criteria which are used in this validation process include school marks, judgment of experts, and acceptable tests. Statistical validation is not often used for teacher-made tests; nevertheless, a teacher certainly must note such data as other school marks and performance on standardized tests for comparison with the performance of examinees on his own tests.

TYPES OF VALIDITY

Because the aims of evaluation differ, a variety of techniques and instruments have been developed to improve evaluation; and for the different types of evaluations, instruments, and techniques different types of validity are necessarily involved. The four categories of validity which are most frequently ascribed to the various evaluation approaches are those of the American Psychological Association: (1) content validity, (2) predictive validity, (3) concurrent validity, and (4) construct validity.

CONTENT VALIDITY.   Content validity refers to the degree to which an instrument samples the subject matter in the area to be measured or the degree to which it coincides with the instructional objectives which are to be measured in a given field. Content validity is a primary consideration in the achievement-testing field, regardless of whether the instrument under consideration is standardized or teacher-made. The content objectives for which measurement instruments are designed are most frequently those which deal with the mastery of specific facts, and thus careful examination of the test items gives an obvious indication of content validity. For this type of validity the examination of text books, courses of study, and the opinions of experts, referred to in discussing curricular validity, are most valuable.

The teacher who wishes to use an achievement test to measure student progress has or should have a definite list of educational objectives in mind. If he is teaching English grammar, he hopes to teach certain fundamental skills in language usage. He may subdivide these skills into specifics such as knowledge of the parts of speech and their functions in sentences, the ability to use commas correctly in punctuating sentences, and the ability to spell correctly all of the words most commonly used in writing and speaking. His specific breakdown of the desirable skills and the relative emphasis or weight which he attaches to these skills will form a useful framework from which he can either construct informal achievement tests having content validity for his class or evaluate standardized tests to be used to measure his objectives.

In judging the content validity of a standardized achievement test, the teacher would do well to read carefully the test manuals accompanying the test under consideration. Most manuals give an extensive discussion of the objectives and coverage of a test as well as the basis on which its validity has been determined. Examination of the manual, however, is insufficient basis for judgment; the analysis of the test in O. K. Buros' *Mental Measurements Yearbook*,[1] which gives unbiased evidence concerning numerous tests, is another valuable source to consult. In the final analysis, however, a detailed item-by-item examination of the achievement tests being considered gives the teacher the best basis for judgment, particularly when the items are tabulated under the teacher's educational objectives in order to determine the relative emphasis and coverage of the test. This procedure is time-consuming but worthwhile. Content validity must also be considered with test types other than the achievement test, e.g., in intelligence and aptitude tests, although in such tests it is a less important consideration than other forms of validity.

OBJECTIVE TESTS.   A major advantage of objective tests is that they can be refined and the items reused so that well-constructed teacher-made tests can be made extremely valid. Furthermore, adaptation of these tests to the teacher's objectives may make them even more valid for his purposes than may be possible with standardized instruments.

The best means of determining the validity of objective tests is to compare the test content to the table of specifications and to the course outline. It is also sometimes helpful to have one's colleagues examine the test and make suggestions for improvement. Pupils too may have suggestions which are helpful, particularly when they can help identify those items which are ambiguous or difficult to understand. Since pupils often write comments after the items which they find confusing, it is wise to consider revising or discarding those items on which several pupils have commented.

Another important step in the evaluation of objective tests is item analysis, a check of internal validity which determines the percent of pupils in the high group and the percent in the slow group who answered each item correctly. In addition to indicating the con-

[1] Buros, Oscar K. (ed.), *The Fifth Mental Measurements Yearbook*, Highland Park, New Jersey, Gryphon Press, 1959.

tribution of separate items to over-all validity, such an analysis also gives information on the difficulty of each item and the discrimination of each item between good and poor pupils. If a higher percent of good pupils than poor pupils answers an item correctly, that item shows positive discrimination.

Since it requires time, item analysis should not be done for tests that are carelessly prepared and which, in the judgment of the teacher, are too easy, too difficult, or weak in discriminating between good and poor pupils. Also there should probably be no fewer than 100 test papers if the item analysis is to be useful.

For teacher-made tests the following simple procedure gives adequate evidence for determining the quality and difficulty of the items:

1. Select the top 20 to 30 percent and the bottom 20 to 30 percent of the papers.
2. Working with one group at a time, place the papers on a large table overlapping each other so that only the response column of each paper is visible.
3. Count the number of correct responses on each item and convert to percents, which are entered on the record sheet. For example, if 18 out of 20 pupils in the high group get the item correct, 90 percent should be entered on the record sheet for the item.
4. When the correct responses have been counted for both the high and low groups on all items, the power of the item can be determined by calculating the percent in both groups who responded correctly. For example, when 32 of the 40 pupils have succeeded on the item, the ease index is 80 percent. Or, stated another way, the difficulty level is 20 percent because 20 percent failed the item.
5. Calculate the discrimination of each item by using the following formula:

$$D = \frac{U - L}{N}$$

where D = index of item-discriminating power.
　　　　U = number of pupils in upper group answering item correctly.

L = number of pupils in lower group answering item correctly.

N = number of pupils in each group.

The discrimination index will range from +1.00 to −1.00, and only items which show positive scores will be retained. A discrimination index above +0.40 is desirable.

The very easy items which were answered correctly by all pupils should be discarded, although a few may be retained for use at the beginning of future tests to help establish good test psychology for pupils who fear objective tests. Other items which should be discarded are those which do not discriminate between good and poor pupils or which show negative discrimination—those on which the poorest pupils are more successful than the best pupils.

For multiple-choice test items, the item analysis should include a record of the number of pupils choosing each choice to give some evidence concerning the plausibility of incorrect choices. Items which discriminate properly but have weak distracters can often be rewritten and salvaged for future use. When the individual items are written on cards for filing, item-analysis information should be entered on the cards for future reference.

ESSAY TESTS.   Essay tests cannot be refined and standardized as can objective tests, but they can be evaluated to determine whether they accomplish the measurement task for which they were designed. Essay tests are the most valid measure of objectives such as the pupil's ability to express himself, to apply knowledge in the solution of problems, and to analyze cause-and-effect relationships. The test questions can be re-examined after the test has been administered to determine whether they actually measured such objectives as those above or whether they measured only the kinds of knowledge which could be better measured objectively. Although it is good practice in an essay test to include several questions of the restricted-response type as well as the extended-response type, in order to improve the test sample and the grading reliability, such a practice may, if the questions are not carefully constructed, focus the measurement on behavior objectives which are better adapted to objective-type measurement. If a table of specifications has been constructed and the completed test re-examined by comparing it to the intended purposes listed in the table, measurement will probably be confined principally to the areas best suited for essay tests. Here also it is helpful to submit an essay test to critical evaluation by one's colleagues to be certain that the questions are clearly stated so that pupils can be expected to confine their answers to the intended areas.

PERFORMANCE TESTS.   The two most helpful bases for comparison in evaluating performance instruments are the job analysis and the table of specifications. Comparing the completed instruments against these two outlines will help insure validity as well as help safeguard against loading the instruments too heavily with items which measure only one or two aspects of the job or one or two of the performance objectives.

Since performance measurement is primarily concerned with how well a pupil actually applies his knowledge in practical job performance, the ultimate indication of the validity of the measuring instrument will be predictive, through a follow-up of the pupils and a correlation of job success with class grades (see discussion of predictive validity below).

ORAL EXAMINATIONS.   If an oral examination is long enough to require a table of specifications, the completed examination can be compared to the table for evaluation. Otherwise the examination probably emphasizes instructional rather than measurement purposes, and it can be evaluated on the basis of its relative instructional effectiveness rather than on the basis of the measurement which results.

PREDICTIVE VALIDITY.   High predictive validity is present in an evaluative instrument or technique if relative success of the student can be predicted accurately from the score or rating obtained. Certainly a major aim of education is to modify student behavior in a way that will contribute to his present and future success. Some of the testing instruments which teachers normally use are specifically designed for a predictive purpose. This is the case with aptitude tests and to a somewhat lesser degree with personal-adjustment inventories, interest inventories, and intelligence tests. Confidence in the predictive validity of the instrument is displayed when students are grouped in classes on the basis of their IQs, when they are refused admittance to college on the basis of entrance scores, when they are given a teacher recommendation for a job on the basis of class grades, or when as adults they are selected for civil-service jobs on the basis of examinations. Confidence in the predictive validity of the technique is evident when a teacher is selected for a job on the basis of an interview, of credentials, or of a written job application. In each of these cases the sometimes fallacious assumption is made that successful performance in the one instance forecasts success in the somewhat different task. Unfortunately, success in complex jobs such as teaching is rarely so easily forecast, for skill in paper-and-pencil tasks does not transfer as well as we would wish to actual job performance, and subjective judgments of evaluators such as those involved in interviewing are often fallacious or unduly influenced by unimportant factors.

In determining the predictive validity of an instrument, follow-up of the pupils who have been evaluated is necessary. In a broad sense the predictive validity of the school itself is involved in cases where follow-up studies of graduates and drop-outs are conducted for the purpose of determining the fitness of the school's program to equip students for success in postschool life. More frequently, however, the predictive validity of a specific evaluative instrument is determined through the use of correlation. The test scores of a group of students on an aptitude test may be statistically correlated with grades in the courses for which aptitude was checked, or the aptitude scores may be correlated with the scores which the same group of pupils subsequently made on a standardized achievement test. A high relationship between the two sets of scores indicates high predictive validity. It should be pointed out, however, that scholastic aptitude tests and specific aptitude tests often measure very much the same subject matter as the achievement tests in the same areas, so that students who do well on the one type of test will also do well on the other type. Perhaps as good an indication as any of predictive validity is the success criterion of the test subjects: do the students who receive high scores in a music-aptitude test succeed as musicians and those who receive low scores fail? There are predictive statistical techniques which are currently used successfully to predict group performance, and fairly accurate predictions are also made for individual performance; however, these techniques require more advanced statistical knowledge than is appropriate for this text.

CONCURRENT VALIDITY.   A teacher's educational objectives are often of such a nature that their achievement cannot be measured directly but must be inferred or measured indirectly. Concurrent validity is a characteristic which the measuring instrument or evaluative technique must have in order to determine the current status of a pupil; it is concerned with present student behavior. For example, in the area of English grammar an important objective is that of developing in students the ability to write correctly according to grammatical rules. Those pupils who score well in an achievement test should also write and speak correctly in their everyday use of the language, if the concurrent validity of that test is high. Some of the same difficulties incurred in determining predictive validity are also present in concurrent validity, with the alleviating factor that present status is easier to determine than future because the pupils are physically present to be observed.

CONSTRUCT VALIDITY.   In psychology the term *construct* refers to certain discrete, identifiable human characteristics, such as boldness, dominance, and insecurity. Construct validity is particularly important in personality tests but is not usually relevant to teacher-made tests.

RELIABILITY

The second important quality of a measuring instrument is its reliability, or consistency. A reliable instrument is one which is consistent enough that subsequent measurements give approximately the same numerical status to the thing or person being measured.

If a reliable test is given two or three times to the same group, each person in the group should get approximately the same score on all tests. In a sense reliability is a part of validity, for the test with high validity—the test which measures what it purports to measure—should measure that quality with consistency and accuracy. It would be possible, however, to have an extremely reliable test which had very little validity for the purpose for which it was being used. For instance, an algebra test might be reliable but lack validity if it were used in an English class to measure achievement in grammar.

The accuracy or consistency of measurement is subject to errors which are inherent in the instrument or in the technique of applying the instrument, but it is also conditioned by pupil error. A reliable instrument which is unskillfully administered might get unreliable test results, just as the same instrument could become unreliable if the pupils performed unreliably because of poor motivation, lack of interest, environmental problems, illness, or many other factors. Reliability is somewhat easier to check than validity, and one of several correlation approaches may be used to check the coefficient of reliability. Because of the nature of the errors listed above, three different types of reliability coefficients are often obtained: (1) coefficient of stability, (2) coefficient of equivalency, and (3) coefficient of internal consistency. The determination of each of these types requires a different method.

TEST-RETEST METHOD

With the test-retest method only one form of the test is necessary, since the test is given to a group of pupils and after a reasonable lapse of time—one to six months—the same test is given to the same group. The two sets of scores are then correlated statistically to determine reliability. The test-retest method gives a *coefficient of stability* because it is based on the stability of the performance of a group of students in a retest situation after a lapse of time following the first administration of the test. This method is subject to some weakness since it is readily apparent that the pupils will have changed somewhat during the period intervening between the first and second testing. As the amount of change in individual pupils will vary, it is impossible to determine whether score differences are a result of low test reliability or of marked pupil change. For example, a certain pupil has high intelligence, but he lacks interest in the subject and does poorly on the first test. During the intervening period, however, he has had some experiences which spark an intense interest, causing him to devote considerably more time than the rest of the class to the subject. It is apparent that this pupil will show a great change in score when he takes the test a second time.

The matched-group technique is rarely used except for experimental purposes, since it is seldom possible to get two large groups matched on the basis of several criteria. With this method only one test form is necessary, since the same test can be given to both groups at the same time and the scores of matched pairs of students can be correlated. The weakness of this method is that it is impossible to be sure whether the difference in scores between the two groups is the result of matching error or of low test reliability.

ALTERNATE-FORMS METHOD

With the alternate-forms method two equivalent forms of a test are made up and a group of pupils is given both forms in order that their scores on each form can be compared. If the two sets of scores show a high degree of relationship, or a high correlation, the test is said to be reliable. Obviously the higher the correlation, the more reliable the test will be.

The alternate-forms method gives a *coefficient of equivalency* if both forms of the test are administered to the same group of pupils at the same time, since the purpose of the method is to develop two forms on which pupils obtain equivalent scores and equivalent rank within their group. Both the equivalency of the test forms and the stability of the group of pupils may be checked if the second form of the test is administered some time later than the first form, the amount of lapsed time determining the group stability.

Although the alternate-form reliability coefficient may be somewhat lower than that obtained by other methods, it is a valuable method because of the obvious classroom usefulness of having more than one equivalent form of a test that will give a recheck of either group or individual test results.

SPLIT-HALF METHOD

The split-half method of determining reliability is used more than any other method because it requires only one group of pupils, one test form, and one test administration. With this method the Spearman-Brown formula given below is commonly used, and the pupils' scores on the even-numbered test items are correlated against their scores on the odd-numbered items. This technique actually gives a *coefficient of internal consistency* in that it compares the rank and score of pupils on one half of the test against their rank and score on the other half. Since this splitting technique has in effect divided the test into two short tests, and reliability is affected adversely by shortening, the following Spearman-Brown formula is used to obtain an estimate of reliability for the entire test:

$$r_{xx} = \frac{2r_{oe}}{1 + r_{oe}}$$

where

r_{xx} = coefficient of internal consistency of the total test.
r_{oe} = coefficient of correlation between pupils' odd-half scores and their even-half scores.

The application of this formula is illustrated by an achievement test in English in which the correlation between the odd-half scores of pupils and their even-half scores is 0.85. The coefficient of internal consistency is then

$$r_{xx} = \frac{2\,(0.85)}{1 + 0.85} = 0.92$$

Thus the increase in the coefficient of correlation from 0.85 for the split halves to 0.92 for the total test indicates the gain to be expected by lengthening the test.

When an item analysis has been run on a test and the difficulty value or the proportion of pupils responding correctly to each item has been obtained, the following Kuder-Richardson formula may be used for calculating internal consistency:

$$r_{xx} = \left(\frac{N}{N-1}\right)\left(1 - \frac{\Sigma pq}{s_t^2}\right)$$

where

N = number of items.

p = proportion (percent of pupils answering item correctly).

$q = 1 - p$.

s_t^2 = standard deviation of total test squared.

Although the Kuder-Richardson formula is also calculated on one test form, as is the Spearman-Brown formula, the Kuder-Richardson approach gives the additional information of item and test difficulty.

Of the methods discussed, the alternate-forms method is most useful to the person administering the test. It is important to have more than one form of a test with high reliability because, in many instances, several pupils may have to be retested when their first scores are questionable because of illness or any other extenuating circumstance.

FACTORS AFFECTING RELIABILITY

Controllable factors which operate to increase or decrease the relia-bility of a measuring instrument include: (1) the length of the in-strument, (2) the variability of the tested group, (3) the age range of the tested group, (4) the testing conditions, and (5) the objec-tivity of scoring.

LENGTH OF THE INSTRUMENT.   Tests must be short enough to be practical and yet long enough to be reliable. Within limits, length-ening a test has the effect of increasing reliability, provided that the items added are equal to or better in quality than those in the orig-inal test. There is undoubtedly a point of diminishing returns where the test becomes so long that fatigue, boredom, or other factors tend to reduce reliability. Some teachers make a practice of giving short daily quizzes, such as a ten-item true-false quiz. Such short quizzes are completely unreliable as measuring devices unless the scores on four or five such quizzes are accumulated to give one score, in which instance the cumulative test is long enough to give measurement reliability. A true-false test of fewer than about 40 items is too unreliable to have much measurement use.

VARIABILITY OF THE TESTED GROUP.   If a test is administered to an extremely homogeneous group of pupils, the differences between individuals could be so small that a very slight increase or decrease in score would change one person's group rank significantly. Furthermore, if the test is too easy, the variability of scores is reduced and reliability may be effected. For example, if the lowest score for 35 pupils on a test of 100 items is 90 and the highest score is 100, score reliability in a retest situation could be drastically affected since it would be quite possible for the lowest-scoring pupil, whose score was 90, to be ranked near the top in the retest by increasing his score slightly to the middle or high 90s. This example is, of course, hypothetical, but it serves by its exaggeration to show that test reliability is greatest with an unselected heterogeneous group which approximates the normal curve in variability. Even in such a heterogeneous group, however, specific scores of individuals in the middle of the group are less reliable than those of individuals at the extreme because of the phenomenon of concentration of cases at the mean and sparsity at the extremes. The middle of the curve is much like the hypothetical case cited above: slight changes of score result in significant changes of rank.

AGE RANGE OF THE TESTED GROUP.   Although the age range is a factor in standardized tests, teacher-made tests which are administered to one class or grade level are little affected by it because ordinarily there is not a great variability in age range.

TESTING CONDITIONS.   Testing conditions affect reliability in that poor testing environment, including such factors as poor light, ventilation, or heat, can effect the reliability by increasing the human error in the respondents.

OBJECTIVITY OF SCORING.   A test can be inherently reliable but have its reliability reduced either through error or subjectivity in the scoring. The more objective the test the greater the scoring reliability, for objectivity in a test eliminates the personal opinion or judgment of the scorer. Objective tests have the most objective scoring, hence the greatest reliability; however, other test forms will have improved reliability when good scoring keys are prepared and followed carefully.

USABILITY

Usability is the third desirable quality of tests. For a test to have a high degree of usability it should: (1) be easy to administer, (2) be easy to score, (3) be economical to use, both in terms of teacher time and of materials required, (4) have good format, and (5) have meaningful norms.

The usability of a teacher-made test can be insured by observing the following rules:

1. *Have the test typed and duplicated so that each pupil will have a copy.* The copies of the test should have large, clear print on good-quality paper, and the stencils should always be proofread before the tests are duplicated.

2. *Directions to the pupil should accompany each part of the test.* These directions should be explicit in indicating the mode of response and should be simple enough for all to understand.

3. *The test should be designed to fit the time limits of the class period.* Teachers frequently make tests either too long or too short. The test which is too long frustrates the pupil; the test which is too short may give inadequate sampling of learning.

4. *The test should be set up so that it can be readily scored.* In the upper grades and the secondary school, answer sheets may be used, and prepared keys or scoring stencils will facilitate the scoring of most tests.

5. *Care should be exercised in planning the test to make it economical in terms of time required for test construction, duplication, and scoring.* Teaching requires a great deal of time; and although the evaluation of learning is an essential element in good teaching, it should not become so burdensome as to usurp necessary lesson-planning time.

6. *Norms of pupil performance should be established from test results.* Teachers who have kept records of the performances of their previous classes on specific tests or test items have a scale against which to compare the performance of their current classes. Such comparisons are much preferable to the subjective judgment of the teacher in determining the quality of a class's test performance.

SUGGESTED READINGS

AHMANN, J. STANLEY, MARVIN D. GLOCK, and HELEN L. WARDEBERG, *Evaluating Elementary School Pupils,* Boston, Allyn and Bacon, 1960, 435 pp.

Chapter 10 includes information on how to evaluate and improve informal achievement tests.

BARON, DENIS, and HAROLD W. BERNARD, *Evaluation Techniques for Classroom Teachers,* New York, McGraw-Hill, 1958, 297 pp.

Chapter 2 discusses the criteria of measuring instruments with specific reference to standardized instruments, although the criteria discussed also apply to teacher-made instruments.

BEAN, KENNETH LAMONT, *Construction of Educational and Personnel Tests,* New York, McGraw-Hill, 1953, 231 pp.

Chapter 7 contains an excellent but fairly technical discussion of test evaluation, particularly valuable for those with some testing background. Chapter 8 discusses validity and reliability, as well as the problem of establishing norms.

FURST, EDWARD J., *Constructing Evaluation Instruments,* New York, Longmans, Green, Courtesy McKay, 1958, 334 pp.

Chapter 13 has an excellent discussion of the analysis and revision of objective tests, but it gives no consideration to other test forms.

GERBERICH, J. RAYMOND, HARRY A. GREENE, and ALBERT N. JORGENSEN, *Measurement and Evaluation in the Modern School,* New York, McKay, 1962, 622 pp.

Chapter 3 has a good discussion of the various characteristics of a good measurement instrument.

REMMERS, H. H., N. L. GAGE, and J. FRANCIS RUMMEL, *A Practical Introduction to Measurement and Evaluation,* New York, Harper, 1960, 370 pp.

Chapter 5 considers the criteria for evaluating measurement instruments and their use in selecting appropriate instruments for the measurement task.

TRAXLER, ARTHUR E., ROBERT JACOBS, MARGARET S. SELOVER, and AGATHA TOWNSEND, *Introduction to Testing and the Use of Test Results in Public Schools*, New York, Harper, 1953, 113 pp.

WOOD, DOROTHY ADKINS, *Test Construction*, Columbus, Ohio, Merrill, 1960, 134 pp.

Chapter 9 is devoted to the item analysis of objective tests.

CHAPTER 8

Scoring, grading, and assignment of course marks

No testing program is any more effective than the uses to which the results are put in the instructional program. Before test results can be usefully employed in instruction, however, the tests must be scored and grades assigned. Although the scoring of tests has been touched upon in previous chapters, the focus of this chapter is on the methods of scoring and grading, and on the assignment of grades and course marks.

SCORING TESTS

Scoring refers to the process of correcting tests and assigning numerical scores. These scores are generally called *raw scores*, and they indicate the number of items which pupils have answered correctly. In addition, there are also *derived scores*, such as percentiles and standard scores, which are statistically calculated from the raw scores.

Not all types of tests are scored in the same manner. For example, the essay test may either be scored by the point-score method or be subjectively evaluated by the sorting method. The objective test is scored by counting the number of correct responses. Oral and performance examinations may be scored or evaluated with the aid of checklists or rating scales.

OBJECTIVE TESTS

Objective tests can be scored the most quickly and accurately of all the test types. If an answer sheet is used for the test, a scoring key can be made by punching out the correct responses on a cardboard sheet which fits over the answer sheets in such a way that the pupils' errors can be marked through the holes in the cardboard. For short objective tests many teachers find it convenient to memorize the key before beginning to mark the papers. The only difficulty with memorizing the key is that it introduces into the scoring an additional possibility of error.

In true-false and multiple-choice tests pupils have a chance to guess the correct answer; therefore teachers must decide whether or not to use a correction formula to compensate for guessing. If the guessing-correction factor is used, the formula is: Score = Rights — Wrongs/$(N-1)$, where N is the number of choices in the item. Thus for a 40-item true-false test on which a pupil answers 30 items correctly and misses 10 items, the score is 20 $(30-10/1=20)$. Using the same formula for a multiple-choice test with 5 choices on each item, a pupil who answers 30 items correctly and misses 10 items on a 40-item test receives a score of 28 $(30-10/4=27.5,$ or 28). Since guessing is a significant factor in true-false tests, it is desirable to use the correction for guessing in scoring such tests; however, the reduced possibility for guessing the correct response makes the value of the correction formula questionable for multiple-choice tests.

ESSAY TESTS

The scoring of essay tests is discussed in detail in Chapter 5, but it is worth noting again that the serious weakness of the essay test is the general unreliability resulting from the scoring or grading of the test. Carefully prepared keys which can be followed in scoring the test will markedly improve the reliability. In addition, use of either of the two methods discussed in Chapter 5, the point-score method or the sorting method, further improves the reliability. There is no doubt that careless, cursory reading by the evaluator and lack of clearly defined grading criteria have been major factors contributing to the unreliability of the essay test.

PERFORMANCE TESTS

Since there are several types of performance tests, the methods of scoring these tests vary. Objective-type performance tests, such as the identification test, can be scored in the same manner as the conventional objective test. Usually the work-sample test can also be set up so that it can be scored numerically; when a specified number of points is allotted to each work-sample station, pupils' scores can be compiled and handled in the conventional manner.

When pupil products are evaluated, however, the scoring procedure is different in that checklists and rating scales are used to increase the objectivity of the evaluation. Use of the rating scale yields a numerical score which can be either averaged or totaled, as illustrated in the following example of the rating given a pupil on a speech presented in a speech class. If the evaluator uses a rating scale which includes 5 criteria to be rated from 0 to 4 points each, and the pupil receives respective ratings of 3, 2, 2, 3, and 4 for a total score of 14 points, 2.8 is his average score $(14 \div 5 = 2.8)$. The maximum total score which he could have received would have been 20 points, and the maximum average would have been 4 points. His final grade could then be assigned on the basis of his total points, using conventional methods such as fixed standards or curve-grading. If the evaluator prefers to use the average-point system, he can assign letter-grade equivalents by setting up a scale in which 4 points = A, 3 points = B, 2 points = C, 1 point = D, and 0 points = F. The pupil with a 2.8 average would thus receive a B grade, since his average is only slightly less than 3 points.

GRADING TESTS

Just as aversion to the task of grading is characteristic of many teachers, mistrust of grades and examinations is characteristic of pupils ranging from the intermediate grades to the university level. In fact, teachers returning to campuses as summer-session students often seem to have even less confidence in grading standards than do the regular college students—possibly fearing that the sins of their past teaching year will be visited upon them as they assume the pupil role. And it must be granted that the university professor often does little better in grading than does his public school colleague. The remainder of this chapter is focused on some of the problems of grading which have led to this mistrust on the part of pupils.

PROBLEMS OF GRADING

Although teachers are more familiar with the problems of grading than with their solutions, several of the most persistent problems are listed here as the basis for a point of attack in solving them.

1. Course marks frequently do not reflect the actual course achievement of individual pupils.
2. Teachers lack objective, clearly defined criteria for assigning marks.
3. The halo effect frequently influences teachers to grade those whom they like higher than their achievement warrants.
4. Occasionally personality conflicts between a pupil and his teacher cause the pupil to be unfairly penalized when he is assigned a mark.
5. There is a tendency for male teachers to assign higher marks to female pupils than to male pupils for comparable achievement, and the reverse sex bias is also distinguishable in the marks assigned by female teachers.
6. Marks are often given on the basis of insufficient data concerning the achievement of pupils.

Several of these problems can be overcome readily by the teacher if he is aware of them. For example, problems 3, 4, and 5 will be of little concern to the teacher who consciously guards against them.

The first problem mentioned in the list is not easily solved, although the teacher who follows the steps suggested for planning the various types of tests which he uses for measuring pupil achievement will certainly be in a better position to give course grades which reflect the actual achievement of each pupil in his class.

The lack of sufficient criteria and the lack of objective data for marking, noted in problems 2 and 6, are given further consideration later in this chapter.

GENERAL PRINCIPLES OF GRADING

Before the specific methods of grading are considered, it might be well to mention some general principles which teachers should follow when assigning marks to pupils.

In order that marks may truly reflect the learning which took place in a class, *they should be based on the actual class achievement of each pupil in the class.* In others words, a mark should tell a pupil how successful he has been in achieving the goals or behavior objectives of the class and in mastering the content areas studied. His mark should be based on his achievement within the class and not on material or achievement which preceded his enrollment in the present class. This fact has both teaching and measurement implications in that good teaching requires a teacher to assess the background of pupils as they begin the year with him and then to proceed to build on that background, expecting higher standards to be reached by those who begin with a good knowledge of the field than by those with limited backgrounds.

Certainly implied in the principle above is the corollary that *class marks should not be used for disciplinary purposes.* Teachers who occasionally lower the marks of pupils who create disciplinary problems or who are absent from class too many times actually do little to solve the disciplinary problems and they distort the pupils' concept of the achievement which their grades are supposed to represent.

Furthermore, there are more effective ways to correct disciplinary infractions.

In order for pupils to work effectively toward improving their grades, *they should be acquainted with the grading method which the teacher is using*. They should know which factors will be weighed in grading and their relative importance. As a related concept, pupils certainly should be familiar with the course objectives, since these are the basis for both the instruction and the measurement in an effectively conducted classroom.

As a likely aid to achievement, pupils should be permitted to know their grade progress throughout the term. Tests should be returned to pupils and discussed so that they can use their errors as a basis for improvement. Grades may also be posted periodically. To prevent pupils from looking up the grades of their classmates, each pupil can be assigned a number, then if they choose to compare grades, they will have to agree among themselves to tell their numbers to one another.

If the grades are to have comparability from one class to another within a school system, *it is essential that there be staff consensus on the grading policy*. Although there will be some variation in the manner in which individual teachers implement the policy, there should be agreement on the method of reporting marks, the method of assigning marks (curve, fixed standard, etc.), and the relative weight of final examinations. If some such agreement is not arrived at by group discussion among the faculty, there will be a persistent problem of difference in grading standards because some faculty members may set unreasonably high standards, while others at the opposite extreme may hold virtually no standard and pass all pupils regardless of their achievement. Such difference in grade standards confuses pupils, lowers their morale, and may lead to interstaff antagonism harmful to the educational quality of the school.

Unless a teacher is teaching in an atypical community, it is probable that his classes will have approximately a normal-curve variation in intellectual ability; therefore *grade distribution should not vary significantly from the normal-curve percentages*. (See discussion of normal curve on pp. 110–112.) There are, of course, several instances in which significant variation from the normal-curve distribution is justified. Occasionally teachers get classes which are either considerably slower or considerably brighter than typical classes. In these classes the percent of failures or the percent of high grades will probably vary from the normal cure. In secondary schools selective dropout reduces the variability of the junior and senior classes. Thus instructors may expect a higher level of performance of these groups and may give a slightly skewed grade distribution with somewhat higher percentages of high grades than they would give in an unselected, normal group. Elective courses also introduce a selective factor; in these courses the instructor has the choice of setting a higher single standard that he would hold for a normal, unselected group or of skewing his grade distribution to fit the selective population of his class.

In typical, unselected classes in elementary and secondary schools, an excessive rate of failure or an excessive proportion of high grades may indicate poor teaching or a warped sense of grade standards. Some teachers mistakenly believe that good teaching demands high standards with consequent high failure rates. These teachers fail to understand that holding grade standards which only the bright can achieve subverts the whole concept of universal education to which public schools are committed. Slower children will continue to attend school until they reach the age of 16 years, and the good teacher will set reasonable standards which challenge these pupils but which do not eliminate them, force them to cheat, or frustrate them to the extent that they stop trying to learn.

METHODS OF GRADING

The methods of grading which a teacher uses are often the methods which his own teachers used, and he may be completely unfamiliar with the variety of other grading methods which can be used. It is necessary that a teacher be familiar with the numerous methods of grading, and it is probably desirable that he use more than one of the methods in his classes. The methods discussed in this chapter are classified as those based on: (1) an individual standard, (2) a fixed standard, and (3) a group standard.

In the process of assigning course marks, one or all of these methods may be used for grading specific tests or assignments. Although marking in the lower elementary grades is often based on the variable standard of individual pupil capacities rather than on a single fixed standard, the reports to parents frequently are of an informal nature, utilizing such techniques as parent-teacher conferences and written anecdotal reports rather than report cards. Even when grades are reported, they generally are not letter grades but rather evaluations indicating "satisfactory" or "unsatisfactory" achievement. In the upper elementary grades and secondary schools, however, the practice of requiring that a letter grade be reported for each course has encouraged teachers to utilize either fixed and/or group standards for grading the tests and assignments which are weighed in the course mark which they report. Thus the following elaboration of these three bases for grading applies more to the upper than to the lower grades.

INDIVIDUAL STANDARD.   Grading based on an individual standard is sometimes referred to as ability-grading. With this method of grading an effort is made through a standardized testing program to determine each pupil's relative capacity for learning, and a standard of achievement appropriate to that potential is set for each pupil in the class. Thus for a comparable grade less achievement is expected of a dull pupil than of a bright pupil. Performance which would earn an A grade for a dull pupil might be worth only a D grade for a bright pupil. If this method of grading is to be used successfully, it must be understood and accepted by the pupils and their parents. The use of this method also requires the teacher to test carefully at the beginning and at the end of the term to determine how much growth there has been in the interim. With this method pupils are graded on the basis of learning which they have achieved as related to their total learning capacity, rather than on the basis of a single fixed standard of performance.

FIXED STANDARD.   The great majority of American teachers employ some type of fixed standard in assigning grades. With fixed-standard grade assignment, grades are assigned on the basis of subject matter standards which are set by the teacher and which represent, in his judgment, appropriate levels of competence. The most frequently used method for assigning grades is to convert the raw scores into percent scores and assign letter-grade equivalents. Thus a pupil who answers correctly 45 out of 50 test items has a raw score of 45, a percent score of 90, and a letter grade of B. The standard implied by a 70-percent passing mark should not be considered a fixed or unchanging standard, but rather the standard should vary according to the difficulty of the test and the teacher's concept of how difficult the subject should be.

The fixed-standard basis for grading has the advantage that it gives a generally understood meaning to the competence levels which the different letter grades given in a course imply. Teachers, parents, and future employers feel that they understand what a grade of A or B in a course such as algebra means when the fixed-standard grading basis has been used. Nevertheless, there is considerable confusion among those who expect a certain competence of pupils who have received certain grades, because there is actually no consensus on the standards which should be held for each letter grade. But even though consensus does not exist, there is a general feeling among both laymen and educators that they know what an A grade means in terms of pupil competence.

Without intending to repudiate the basis on which the grades of most instructors, from the upper grades through the university, are assigned, two weaknesses of the fixed-standard method should be mentioned. First, the standards are variable in that they are actually set by individual teachers; any teacher can, at the caprice of personal whim, change the standards in his class without the immediate consequence of more than minor repercussions. If he lowers the standards to give a larger number of high grades, parents and pupils will be happy, although a pupil may later be shocked to realize in more advanced work with other teachers that his supposed competence is a fantasy and that he is ill-prepared to continue in the field. Conversely, when an instructor raises his standards so that he gives few high grades and many low grades, he can be fairly certain that his good pupils will succeed in subsequent courses, but he may also at the same time exclude some average pupils who could continue successfully.

As a means of eliminating some of the subjectivity inherent in the percent system of grading, some teachers establish standards or norms based on the performance record of their previous classes. Standards can also be set in terms of levels of subject matter competency if the tests given to each group are comparable in coverage and difficulty. In fact, some objective tests may be reused with several groups of pupils to insure comparability in the measuring instrument. When a test is reused, however, the teacher must be careful to prevent pupils from obtaining copies ahead of time and thus invalidating the estimate of achievement and changing the norms.

Second, the fixed-standard grading basis totally ignores the oft-quoted but seldom implemented concept that education should be adapted to the needs, interests, and abilities of the individual pupil. If a teacher's standards are fixed and inflexible, it is certain that the intellectual caliber of his classes through the years will vary so that in some high-caliber classes he will be forced to give many high grades, and he will have to fail many pupils in other years when the classes are poor.

GROUP STANDARD.   With group-standard grade assignment the individual pupil's achievement is compared to his group or class rather than judged against a rigid set of subject matter standards. With this method either the normal curve or the calculated curve is used as the basis for assigning grades. The group basis for grading permits flexibility of standards to fit the intellectual level of the group. A disadvantage of this basis is that it tends to overemphasize competition which arises when pupils vie with one another for the top ranks within the group.

To assign grades on the normal curve, the teacher arranges the test scores in rank order from the highest to the lowest score and gives the top 7 percent A's and the bottom 7 percent F's. The 24 percent below the top group are given B's and the 24 percent above the bottom group are given D's. The remaining 38 percent in the middle are given C's. This system works well with unselected classes which have approximately the same intellectual variability as that represented by the normal curve.

The contrast in grade distributions for three classes of varying ability when marks are assigned according to fixed standards and on the basis of a normal curve are shown in Fig. 8.1. With the normal curve all three classes receive the same percent of A's, B's, C's, D's, and F's, whereas with fixed standards there are no A's in Class Y or Class Z, and half of Class Z receive F's. Although both systems have been used with classes similar to the three in Fig. 8.1, it is apparent that neither system is satisfactory for all types of classes. Many classes show a distribution different from the normal curve. Any teacher who has taught for a number of years realizes that classes vary. Some are fast, some are slow, and some are quite homogeneous. Therefore it is an injustice to the deviant classes to force their grades into a normal grade distribution which does not represent their true achievement.

In order to meet this difficulty some teachers prefer to calculate the class curve for each test which they administer and then assign grades on the basis of the obtained mean and standard deviation (the calculation of both of these statistics is explained in Chapter 9). Using this procedure makes it possible to avoid the problem of attempting to force a normal grade distribution for a class which is decidedly deviant. When this procedure is followed, a considerably higher than normal percent of A and B grades will be assigned in a bright class, and, conversely, higher percentages of D's and F's will be assigned if a class is slow.

A comparison is shown in Fig. 8.2 between the normal-curve grade distribution and the grade distribution which could result in a bright class when the test scores are decidedly skewed and the grades are assigned from the calculated mean and standard deviation. If this bright class were forced into a normal-curve grade distribution, only 31 percent would receive A and B grades, whereas if they were

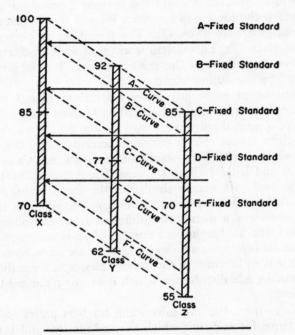

100 ───	A—Fixed Standard
92	B—Fixed Standard
	A- Curve
	B- Curve
85	85 ─── C—Fixed Standard
	C- Curve
77	D—Fixed Standard
	D- Curve
70 Class X	70 ─── F—Fixed Standard
	F- Curve
62 Class Y	
55 Class Z	

Fixed Standard	Normal Curve
A = above 94%	A = 7% of the cases
B = 86–94	B = 24% of the cases
C = 78–85	C = 38% of the cases
D = 70–77	D = 24% of the cases
F = below 70%	F = 7% of the cases

FIG. 8.1. *Comparison of Grade Distribution for Three Classes on a Difficult 100-Item Objective Test, Using Fixed Standards and Curves.*

assigned grades on the basis of calculated mean and standard deviation, their superior performance would be rewarded with 50 percent A and B grades. The group basis of grading using percentile rank or standard scores (see Chapter 9) also permits the teacher some leeway in standards and thus gives pupils in slow groups a better chance of achieving passing marks.

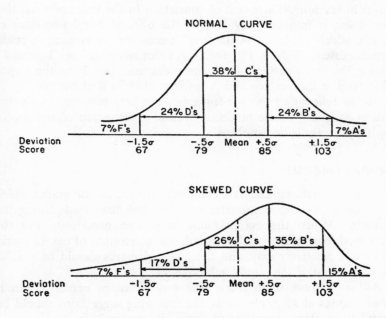

FIG. 8.2. *Curve Grade Distribution.*

It should be noted, however, that superior test performance is not always an indication that a class is superior, for it is possible that the test is much too easy. Therefore it is necessary for the teacher to examine the standardized achievement and intelligence tests of his class and not rely totally on his own experience in judging the intellectual level of the group.

ASSIGNMENT OF COURSE MARKS

Twice a year at the close of the semesters, instruction in American schools stops briefly while teachers administer final examinations and make out semester grades to send home to parents. Many teachers feel that assigning a course mark is one of the most trying tasks in teaching. Their lack of conviction in the value of what they are doing is frequently evident in the offhand but half-serious remarks which are heard in teachers' lounges or workrooms as grades are discussed: "I think I'll give all A's this semester" or "I guess I'll throw the examinations down the stairs and give F to the papers that land at the bottom and A to those that land at the top."

In the following pages are suggestions to help teachers do a better job in assigning course marks, as well as a discussion of the special techniques available to them.

GENERAL PRINCIPLES

A course mark represents a composite picture of the grades which have been given on examinations and of the class work during the semester. When the examinations have been good ones and the class work has been carefully graded, the assignment of course marks should be relatively easy, and the assigned marks should be a valid representation of the pupils' achievement.

Although there is no single best way to assign marks to pupils in all courses at all grade levels, the following suggestions should be useful to teachers regardless of their field or teaching level.

Certainly *teachers should not assign marks without collecting sufficient data about the pupils' achievement to permit a valid judgment to be made.* This principle requires that the teacher administer frequent tests during the grading period, that he give numerous written assignments which are carefully graded, and that he keep an accurate record of each pupil's work in his grade book. In most classes it is also important that the teacher use a variety of types of tests in order to get valid information relating to his teaching objectives, keeping in mind the types of objectives which each type of test is best fitted to measure.

It is important that several achievement factors be weighed in a course mark and that the pupil be aware of the factors to be included as well as their relative weight. Assigning a course mark with a final examination as the sole grading basis gives too limited a picture of achievement. Factors which should normally be weighed in a course mark include: (1) examinations, (2) daily written assignments, (3) review or teaching tests, (4) written research reports, and (5) oral presentations.

The final examination should have a significant weight. In general, the final examination should be assigned a weight of from one-fifth to one-third of the total mark, but the weight should vary according to the course and the objectives of instruction. Since the final examination is so important in measurement, pupils whose grades are high should not be excused from taking it, as they sometimes are in the upper elementary grades and secondary school. The final examination gives the teacher the best single indication of how much each pupil has actually achieved in the course.

USE OF MEDIAN AND MODE

Teachers are most familiar with the arithmetic mean as the basis for assigning the course mark. They average the daily assignments and the examinations, weighing each as they see fit; and woe unto the pupil who has failed to hand in all the assignments, for such occasional lapses of memory may drastically lower his grade. The mean is so strongly influenced by deviant scores that the very good but slightly forgetful pupil who earns the following seven scores—100, 95, 95, 90, 85, 80, and 0—would get an average score of only 78. This low score is unquestionably a poor representation of the caliber of the pupil's achievement, since his completed work is of A or B caliber but his mark based on the mean will probably be C. Some teachers avoid this difficulty by eliminating one or two of the pupil's lowest scores from the list to be averaged, although they rarely eliminate the deviant high score.

Perhaps a better solution is to rely upon the median rather than the mean as a basis for assigning marks. The median is unaffected by extreme scores because it is the midpoint of the distribution of scores. In the example above the pupil's median grade would be 90, which more truly represents his actual achievement than does the mean of 78. If there are numerous grades to be averaged, the mode, or most frequent score received by the pupil, is also useful, although it is less reliable than the median as a measure of central tendency.

The use of median and mode in the analysis of group data is discussed in Chapter 9.

POINT-SCORE MARK ASSIGNMENT

The point-score technique of assigning course marks is useful in classes from the upper elementary grades through the university. There are alternative methods for calculating marks when using the point-score technique, and the teacher's choice of method will probably be based on whether he wishes to curve the final marks or base the marks on the mean scores. These methods are the cumulative-point score, which may be used with a curve, and the grade-point average, based on the mean.

The *cumulative-point score* method is useful when some of the factors to be included in a final mark are not readily assigned either a letter or numerical grade. For example, the daily class work can quickly be evaluated as "unsatisfactory," "satisfactory," or "superior." The following symbols may be used for these categories: ✔/ for superior, ✓ for satisfactory, and ⊂/ for unsatisfactory. Products or procedures in courses which emphasize performance are often rated on a numerical scale; for example, the maximum score might be ten points and the minimum score zero. Finally, in some classes supplementary outside reading may be suggested, with the pupils being given a certain number of points for each reading which they complete satisfactorily. Figure 8.3 presents the grades which a pupil received during a semester on six daily assignments, two performances, and three examinations. The final examination is weighed four times as heavily as the other examinations to give it a weight of approximately one-fourth of the possible cumulative-point score.

After each pupil's cumulative-point score has been totaled, the mean and standard deviation should be calculated and the final marks assigned on the basis of the calculated curve. If the point totals are posted periodically in the classroom, pupils will be able to determine their relative standing in the class, and the teacher should have no difficulty in justifying the marks to pupils or their parents.

| Daily Assignments | Performances | | Examinations | | Total Points |
			Class	Final	
Maximum grade ✓/ ✓/ ✓/ ✓/ ✓/ ✓/	10	10	A A	A	
Score　3 3 3 3 3 3	10	10	4 4	16	62
Pupil's grades ✓/ ✓ ✓ ✓ ✓ ✓/	8	8	A B	B	
Score　1 2 2 2 2 3	8	8	4 3	12	47

Fig. 8.3. *Example of a Pupil's Cumulative-Point Score Earned During a Grading Period.*

The *grade-point average* method is easier to use than the cumulative-point score method and is a better system to follow in most courses. With this system pupils are given letter grades on all their assignments and examinations, and the letter grades are translated into the following point scale before being averaged: A = 4 points, B = 3 points, C = 2 points, D = 1 points, and F = 0 points. For example, if a pupil's daily grades constitute one grade factor, a written report or research paper a second factor, the midterm examination a third factor, and the final examination a fourth factor, and if he earns grades of A on his daily work, B on his written report, B on his midterm, and C on his final examination, he would have a total of 12 points for a 3-point grade average ($12 \div 4$) and would receive a final course mark of B.

There are numerous ways in which the final course mark may be assigned, but the final mark fails in meaning and validity as a representation of the pupil's achievement in the course when it is influenced by factors other than those expressed in the instructional objectives, for instance, when it is used to discipline the pupil or when it is haphazardly assigned without following a mathematical system that is easily computed and understood. Instead of being a task dreaded by teachers, grading can be a pleasant opportunity to assess achievement and report it in marks which pupils understand to be fair and objective measures of their learning.

SUGGESTED READINGS

CLARK, LEONARD H., and IRVING S. STARR, *Secondary School Teaching Methods*, New York, Macmillan, 1959, 340 pp.
 There is an excellent discussion of marking and reporting to parents in Chapter 12, which is practical and easily understood.

REMMERS, H. H., N. L. GAGE, and J. FRANCIS RUMMEL, A *Practical Introduction to Measurement and Evaluation*, New York, Harper, 1960, 370 pp.
 Chapter 9 gives some very practical suggestions for assigning course marks, including a method of weighing the various factors important in the marks.

STRANG, RUTH, *Reporting to Parents*, New York, Bureau of Publications, Teachers College, Columbia University, 1947, 105 pp.
 This short text gives a comprehensive discussion of methods of reporting course marks, and it includes some discussion of the techniques through which pupil achievement can be ascertained.

THORNDIKE, ROBERT L., and ELIZABETH HAGEN, *Measurement and Evaluation in Psychology and Education*, New York, Wiley, 1955, 575 pp.
 Marking and reporting are discussed in Chapter 17. Specific suggestions for assigning course marks are given on pages 482–488.

WRINKLE, WILLIAM L., *Improving Marking and Reporting Practices*, New York, Rinehart, 1947, 120 pp.
 This textbook includes one of the most comprehensive discussions of the whole problem of marking and reporting.

CHAPTER 9 *Statistical treatment of test data*

The classroom teacher has no need to become a statistician, although he must be familiar with the common mathematical techniques of summarizing and handling the data which he obtains through tests. In addition, he should possess enough knowledge of elementary statistics that he can read research reports intelligently and understand the scores commonly used for standardized tests. Proficiency in these statistical techniques requires a background of no more than seventh-grade arithmetic and an understanding of algebraic computations using positive and negative numbers.

This chapter introduces only those basic statistical techniques necessary for summarizing data in graphs, locating the central tendency of group scores, discovering the variability of a group, and converting test scores to standard scores. A mastery of these relatively simple techniques will permit the teacher to do a professional job of organizing test data so that he can use them for grading or instructional purposes.

UNTABULATED DATA

The series of raw scores which a teacher obtains when he gives a test have little meaning unless they are placed into some kind of orderly arrangement. Actually the two most important facts which the teacher wants to find out about scores are (1) the average performance, or *central tendency,* and (2) the *variability,* or range of the class. When the class is small both of these statistics can be quickly calculated from the untabulated data, although the arrangement of the scores in rank order will probably facilitate the assignment of marks.

Pupil A	Pupil B
95	95
95	95
90	90
85	85
80	0
$\overline{445} \div 5 = 89$ (Mean)	$\overline{365} \div 5 = 73$ (Mean)

Fig. 9.1. *Procedure for Obtaining the Mean for a Small Number of Scores.*

The central tendency of scores is represented by (1) the *mean,* or arithmetic average, (2) the *median,* or midpoint of the series of scores, and (3) the *mode,* or most frequently occurring score. The mean, although greatly influenced by extreme scores, is the most frequently used by teachers and is arrived at simply by totaling the scores and dividing by the number of scores in the group. The mean is often used to average daily grades of pupils. The examples in Fig. 9.1 show the computation of mean with ungrouped data. The scores in this figure represent the daily grades of two pupils. Although both pupils received identical grades on the work handed in, pupil B failed to complete one assignment. This one low grade dropped pupil B's mean grade to 73, which is 16 points below the mean grade of pupil A.

When there are one or two extreme scores which are considerably higher or lower than the rest of the scores to be averaged, the median may give a truer picture of the central tendency. When there is only a small number of scores to work with, the median can be obtained simply by ranking the scores and locating the midpoint, as illustrated in Fig. 9.2.

92	93
91	92
90	91
88	90
← Median = 87	89
86 (There are 4 scores above	88 ← Median = 88
84 and 4 scores below this point.)	87 (There are 5 scores above
80	86 and 5 scores below this point.)
40	85
	80
	50

Fig. 9.2. *Procedure for Determining the Median for a Small Number of Ranked Grades.*

The mode, the most frequently occurring score, is the most easily obtained of the three measures of central tendency. One needs only examine the scores to determine which score is modal, or most frequent. However, the mode is not a reliable measure of central tendency unless there is a large number of scores because it may by chance fall at any point along the scale.

With small numbers of scores variability is best expressed by range. The range is obtained by subtracting the lowest score from the highest score and adding one. For example, if the best pupil in the class had a raw score of 65 on a test and the poorest pupil had a raw score of 30, the range would be $(65 - 30) + 1$, or 36.

FREQUENCY DISTRIBUTION

Teachers usually give a test to a group large enough to make tedious the task of adding the scores and calculating the central tendency by the methods discussed above. In such instances a systematic tabulation of the scores in a frequency distribution provides the teacher with shortcuts in calculating both the measures of central tendency and the measures of variability.

As a typical example, let us assume that the teacher has administered an algebra test to 50 pupils and obtained the raw scores listed below. The highest score is 94 and the lowest is 20, giving a range of

30	71	49	63	86
45	40	58	65	61
40	39	56	68	58
30	45	84	73	91
51	25	56	52	77
39	81	76	48	66
40	64	59	47	67
80	63	30	52	62
59	71	44	71	57
71	38	27	20	53

75. In tabulating the scores in a frequency distribution, it is desirable to have about 15 intervals; thus in this example the interval is 5 (75/5 = 15). After the teacher decides upon the interval, he proceeds to set up the table and tabulate the distribution as illustrated in Fig. 9.3. The bottom interval of the table may begin either with the lowest test score or, as in the illustration, with a number low enough to include the lowest score but divisible by the interval. This second method is somewhat easier for beginners and may help avoid errors in setting up the intervals of the table. The table gives the teacher a short summary of the test results and can readily be translated into graphic form. In fact, when the scores are tabulated on a typewriter, they do show the actual graphic conformation or distribution curve of the group of scores.

Two such typewriter tabular arrangements of these scores are shown in Fig. 9.4. The teacher is probably familiar with the kind of graphic representation shown in Tabulation A since he has encountered similar representations in financial or population studies.

Class Interval	Tabulations	Frequency
90–94	/	1
85–89	/	1
80–84	///	3
75–79	//	2
70–74	NHJ	5
65–69	////	4
60–64	NHJ	5
55–59	NHJ //	7
50–54	////	4
45–49	NHJ	5
40–44	////	4
35–39	///	3
30–34	///	3
25–29	//	2
20–24	/	1
	N = 50	Σf = 50

FIG. 9.3. *Frequency Distribution of the Raw Scores of 50 Pupils on a Teacher-constructed Algebra Test.*

Tabulation B, however, begins to look very much like a conventional graph when it is enclosed with a line accentuating the conformation of the curve.

GRAPHIC PRESENTATION OF TEST RESULTS

Graphs which show the curve of a class distribution are constructed to represent the data on a frequency-distribution table. Two types of graphs are used for this purpose: (1) the frequency polygon, or line graph, and (2) the histogram, or bar graph. If the teacher wishes to portray two sets of test data on the same graph, the frequency

90-94	x
85-89	x
80-84	xxx
75-79	xx
70-74	xxxxx
65-69	xxxx
60-64	xxxxx
55-59	xxxxxxx
50-54	xxxx
45-49	xxxxx
40-44	xxxx
35-39	xxx
30-34	xxx
25-29	xx
20-24	x

TABULATION B

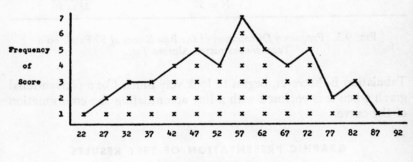

Midpoints of Intervals

FIG. 9.4. *Two Typewriter Tabular Techniques Portraying Data Graphically.*

polygon is the better graph because, by drawing the two lines in different colors, he can get a quick visual comparison of the performance of a class on two different tests. However, if he wishes to present the data so that they can be easily seen by a group of people, the histogram is the better form. Otherwise there is actually little advantage of one graphic form over the other.

FREQUENCY POLYGON

The frequency polygon can be readily constructed if the steps below are followed carefully:

1. Using graph paper with 10 to 20 squares per inch, lay off the base line or X-axis in equal intervals.
2. Label these intervals with the midpoints of each class interval, including one interval below and one above those in which there are scores.
3. Lay off the vertical or Y-axis in equal intervals.
4. Label the units of the Y-axis from zero to the highest number of scores tabulated in any interval of the frequency distribution.
5. Plot the score frequency at each midpoint and connect the points with a line.

Figure 9.5 is an example of a frequency polygon plotted from the 50 algebra scores in Fig. 9.3. It is not always easy to decide how to space the vertical and horizontal axes of the graph, but a good rule of thumb to follow is that the graph should be 4 to 5 inches wide and about two-thirds as tall as it is wide. It is also helpful to center the graph on the page so that the title and any additional pertinent information can be written above and below the figure.

HISTOGRAM

The histogram is constructed in the same manner as the frequency polygon except that instead of plotting the score frequencies at the midpoints of the intervals, the total space represented by each interval and its frequencies is plotted. In Fig. 9.6 a histogram repre-

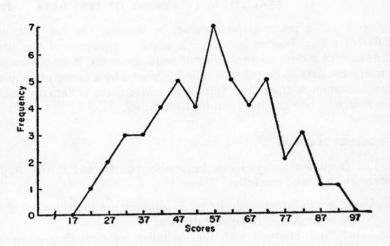

Fig. 9.5. *Frequency Polygon of the 50 Algebra Scores.*

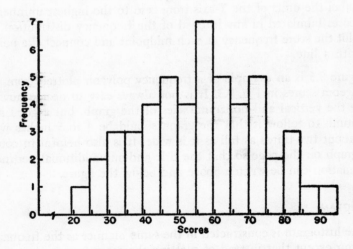

Fig. 9.6. *Histogram of the 50 Algebra Scores.*

sents the same 50 algebra scores shown in the frequency polygon in Fig. 9.5. This change in plotting necessitates labeling the base line of the histogram with either the exact limits of each interval or the lower limit of each interval, instead of labeling with the midpoints as in the frequency polygon. In Fig. 9.7 the method of labeling and plotting is shown for the bottom interval of the frequency distribution.

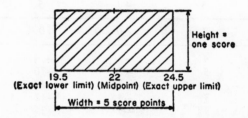

FIG. 9.7. *Method of Labeling and Plotting the Bottom Interval of the Frequency Distribution Shown in Fig. 9.6.*

CENTRAL TENDENCY AND VARIABILITY

Although graphic portrayal of data is useful in helping the teacher see the distribution curve, it is necessary to calculate both central tendency and variability before the data can be adequately interpreted. Perhaps the most functional of the calculation measures are the mean and the standard deviation, both of which may be determined from the frequency distribution.

MEAN: SHORT METHOD

The short method of calculating the mean is used when the scores have been tabulated in the frequency distribution. This method requires the teacher to select an arbitrary reference point, and then calculate the correction which is added to or subtracted from this

Class Intervals	Frequency	Deviation	fd	fd^2
90–94	1	+7	7	49
85–89	1	+6	6	36
80–84	3	+5	15	75
75–79	2	+4	8	32
70–74	5	+3	15	45
65–65	4	+2	8	16
60–64	5	+1	5	5
55–59	7	0	0	0
50–54	4	−1	− 4	4
45–49	5	−2	−10	20
40–44	4	−3	−12	36
35–39	3	−4	−12	48
30–34	3	−5	−15	75
25–29	2	−6	−12	72
20–24	1	−7	− 7	49
	f = 50		Σfd = − 8	Σfd^2 = 562

$$\text{Mean} = 57 + 5 \left(\frac{-8}{50} \right) \qquad \text{Mean} = M' + \left[i \left(\frac{\Sigma fd}{N} \right) \right]$$

$$\text{Mean} = 57 + 5 \ (-.16)$$

$$\text{Mean} = 57 - .80, \text{ or } 56.2$$

$$\sigma = 5 \sqrt{\frac{562}{50} - \left(\frac{-8}{50} \right)^2} \qquad \sigma = i \sqrt{\frac{\Sigma fd^2}{N} - \left(\frac{\Sigma fd}{N} \right)^2}$$

$$\sigma = 5 \sqrt{11.24 - (-.16)^2}$$

$$\sigma = 5 \sqrt{11.22}$$

$$\sigma = 5 \times 3.34, \text{ or } 16.7$$

Fig. 9.8. *Calculation from the Frequency Distribution of Mean and Standard Deviation of the 50 Algebra Scores.*

point, according to whether the point was too low or too high. The formula for the calculation is:

$$\text{Mean} = M' + \left[i \left(\frac{\Sigma fd}{N} \right) \right]$$

where M' = arbitrary reference point.
   i = interval used in the distribution.
   f = number of scores within each interval.
   d = deviation from the arbitrary reference point.
   N = total number of scores in the distribution.

Using this formula with the 50 algebra scores in Fig. 9.8, the mean of 56.2 is obtained.

STANDARD DEVIATION

The mean and the standard deviation are used together, and they are calculated from the same frequency-distribution data. Standard deviation is the most reliable measure of variability and is used as the basis for several types of standard scores, including Z-scores and T-scores. On teacher-made tests the standard deviation varies considerably according to the number of items included on the test and the range in intellectual ability of the group tested. A test with a small number of items will have a small standard deviation even when the group is quite heterogeneous. However, if a good objective power test of 80 to 100 items is given to a typically heterogeneous class, the standard deviation should approximate that of the standardized group intelligence tests, i.e., ranging between 10 and 16 points. Lower standard deviations indicate a small range in ability within the group, and higher standard deviations indicate a great range in ability.

The formula for calculating standard deviation is:

$$\sigma = i \sqrt{\frac{\Sigma fd^2}{N} - \left(\frac{\Sigma fd}{N} \right)^2}$$

where σ = standard deviation.
   i = interval used in the distribution.

Σfd^2 = sum of the squared deviations multiplied by the scores within
each interval.

Σfd = sum of the products of the frequency scores and the deviation
of each interval.

N = total number of scores in the distribution.

Using the formula above, the standard deviation calculated for the
50 algebra test scores in Fig. 9.8 is 16.7, which, with 95 items in the
test, would indicate a fairly typical group if the test were a good one.

STANDARD SCORES

Teachers often wish to compare the scores of a class on several
tests. Unless the scores have been translated into common terms,
such comparisons have little meaning. For example, let us suppose
that a class took an objective English test of 60 items and earned a

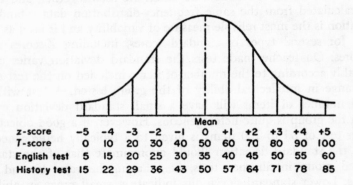

						Mean					
z-score	−5	−4	−3	−2	−1	0	+1	+2	+3	+4	+5
T-score	0	10	20	30	40	50	60	70	80	90	100
English test	5	15	20	25	30	35	40	45	50	55	60
History test	15	22	29	36	43	50	57	64	71	78	85

FIG. 9.9. z-Score and T-Score Equivalents for Teacher-
constructed English and History Tests.

mean score of 35 with a standard deviation of 5. Later the same class
took an objective history test of 85 items and obtained a mean score
of 50 and a standard deviation of 7. One pupil who took both tests
received 40 on the English test and 57 on the history test. By translating these scores into either z-scores or T-scores, the teacher can

find the pupil's position in both of the class distributions as well as his comparative achievement on both tests. Since this pupil is exactly one standard deviation above the mean of his class on both the English and the history test, it is apparent that he achieved comparable scores on both tests. Or in terms of the standard scores in Fig. 9.9, he received a z-score of $+1$ and a T-score of 60 on both tests.

When z-scores are used, a test score is translated into a numerical score, the value of which indicates the number of standard deviations above or below the arithmetic mean which the test score represents. Thus, in the example above, a z-score of $+1$ denotes the position of the test score on the curve of the scores. Although T-scores are similar to z-scores, the T-scores are arranged on a 100-point scale with an arbitrary mean of 50 and an assigned value of 10 points for each standard deviation; hence a T-score of 60 is the equivalent of a z-score of $+1$.

CALCULATED GRADE CURVE

In the discussion of grading in Chapter 8 it was noted that test grades may be assigned on the basis of the normal curve. However, because of the disadvantages of using the normal curve procedure with skewed classes, it is often preferable to assign curve grades on the basis of the calculated curve—using the arithmetic mean and the standard deviation computed from the test to determine the letter grade limits. To assign grades in this manner, one needs simply to locate the mean on the base line of the curve and to mark off $\frac{1}{2}\ \sigma$ above and $\frac{1}{2}\ \sigma$ below to determine the C-range. The B-range extends from $+\frac{1}{2}\ \sigma$ to $+1\frac{1}{2}\ \sigma$; the D-range from $-\frac{1}{2}\ \sigma$ to $-1\frac{1}{2}\ \sigma$; the A's lie above $+1\frac{1}{2}\ \sigma$; and the F's lie below $-1\frac{1}{2}\ \sigma$. The advantage of assigning curve grades on the calculated, rather than the normal, curve is that in skewed classes the grade distribution more nearly represents the ability level of the class. In a bright class a considerably higher percentage of high grades can be given than would be possible with the normal curve. On the other hand, slow classes receive a higher proportion of low grades with this process.

MEDIAN

As pointed out previously, the mean may give a biased measure of central tendency when there are several exceptional scores in the distribution. If the teacher has several either exceptionally dull or exceptionally bright pupils in an otherwise typical class, the mean score of tests will be lowered or raised appreciably by the scores of these few pupils. In such classes the median will give a better picture of central tendency because it will not be influenced by these exceptional scores. The median can be calculated directly from the frequency distribution by using the procedure followed in the calculation of median and Q_1 (see Fig. 9.10):

1. Divide the total number of scores by 2 or multiply by 50 percent to find out how many scores lie on each side of the median $(50 \div 2 = 25)$.
2. Accumulate the scores in each interval by adding from the bottom until the interval in which the median lies is reached. In the example in Fig. 9.10 there are 22 scores below the median interval.
3. Subtract the accumulated scores from the number needed to reach the median $(25 - 22 = 3)$.
4. Calculate the proportion of the median interval needed by multiplying by the interval size the number of scores needed divided by the number of scores in the interval $(3/7 \times 5 = 2.14)$.
5. Add the result of the above calculation to the exact lower limit of the median interval. Thus median $= 54.5 + 2.14$, or 56.6.

All other percentiles are calculated in the same manner as the median, except that the number of scores in step 1 varies according to the percentile which is being located. For example, Q_1, the twenty-fifth percentile, requires 25 percent of the 50 scores, or 12.5.

SEMI-INTERQUARTILE RANGE.   When the median is used to show central tendency, the semi-interquartile range (Q) rather than the stand-

Class Intervals	Frequency	
90–94	1	
85–89	1	
80–84	3	
75–79	2	
70–74	5	
65–69	4	
60–64	5	↑ f_{cum} (Q_3) = 34
55–59	7	
50–54	4	↑ f_{cum} (mdn.) = 22
45–49	5	
40–44	4	
35–39	3	↑ f_{cum} (Q_1) = 9
30–34	3	
25–29	2	
20–24	1	

$$N = 50$$

$$\text{Median} = 54.5 + \left(\frac{\frac{50}{2} - 22}{7} \times 5\right)$$

$$= 54.5 + \left(\frac{3}{7} \times 5\right)$$

$$= 54.5 + 2.14, \text{ or } 56.6 \text{ (median)}$$

$$Q_1 = 39.5 + \left(\frac{12.5 - 9}{4} \times 5\right)$$

$$= 39.5 + \left(\frac{3.5}{4} \times 5\right)$$

$$= 39.5 + 4.4, \text{ or } 43.9 \ (Q_1)$$

FIG. 9.10. *Calculation of the Median and Quartiles for the 50 Algebra Scores.*

ard deviation should be used to show the variability. Q is one-half
the range between the twenty-fifth and the seventy-fifth percentile.

$$Q = \frac{Q_3 - Q_1}{2}$$

For the group of scores in Fig. 9.10,

$$Q = \frac{68.9 - 43.9}{2}, \text{ or } Q = 12.5$$

PERCENTILES

If the teacher chooses to use the median to determine the central
tendency of a group of test scores and Q to determine the variability, he can express the test scores in percentiles if he wishes to compare them to other standardized or teacher-constructed tests. Based

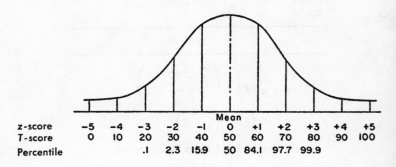

z-score	−5	−4	−3	−2	−1	Mean 0	+1	+2	+3	+4	+5
T-score	0	10	20	30	40	50	60	70	80	90	100
Percentile			.1	2.3	15.9	50	84.1	97.7	99.9		

FIG. 9.11. *Relationship Between Percentiles and Standard Scores.*

upon a 100-point scale, the percentile shows the pupil's rank within
the group; e.g., the pupil whose score falls at the twenty-fifth percentile ranks higher than 25 percent of the pupils who took the test.
The most serious problem with percentiles is that minor score changes
in the middle of the curve change a pupil's percentile rank drastically, whereas large score changes at the lower and upper ends of the
scale effect only minor changes in rank. The relationship between

rcentiles and standard scores is shown in Fig. 9.11. Percentiles are
eful only for expressing those scores located in the range between
ree standard deviations below and three standard deviations above
e mean.

Percentile rank may be approximately determined from the fre-
ency distribution by calculating the percentile rank for the upper
iits of each interval. An example of such a scale is shown for the
algebra test scores in Fig. 9.12.

Class Intervals	Frequency	Cumulative Frequency	Percentile Rank of Upper Limits
90–94	1	50	100
85–89	1	49	98
80–84	3	48	96
75–79	2	45	90
70–74	5	43	86
65–69	4	38	76
60–64	5	34	68
55–59	7	29	58
50–54	4	22	44
45–49	5	18	36
40–44	4	13	26
35–39	3	9	18
30–34	3	6	12
25–29	2	3	6
20–24	1	1	2

FIG. 9.12. *Percentile Rank of the Upper Limits of the Frequency-
Distribution Intervals of the 50 Algebra Scores.*

In conclusion, it should be noted that not all of the statistics dis-
ssed in this chapter are essential for meaningful reporting of test
ults. But if test results are to be compared, it is necessary to select
e measure of central tendency, a related measure of variability,
d related scores. If the mean is selected for central tendency, stand-

ard deviation should be used for variability and test scores should
translated into standard scores. If the median is used, Q and perc
tiles are the appropriate statistics.

SUGGESTED READINGS

DOWNIE, N. M., and R. W. HEATH, *Basic Statistical Methods*, N
York, Harper, 1959, 289 pp.
> The first section of this book gives extended coverage of
> statistical concepts discussed in this chapter.

GARRETT, HENRY E., *Testing for Teachers*, New York, American Bo
1959, 262 pp.
> Chapter 2 and Appendix A discuss the computation and use
> the most important statistics. The computations are clearly explai
> and are accompanied by examples.

GUILFORD, J. P., *Fundamental Statistics in Psychology and Educati*
New York, McGraw-Hill, 1956, 569 pp.
> This is an elementary book in statistics which is particularly u
> ful to the teacher who is mathematically inclined and who wisl
> to learn additional statistical computations with measurement a
> evaluation data.

MANUEL, HERSCHEL T., *Elementary Statistics for Teachers*, New Yo
American Book, 1962, 213 pp.
> This text uses the combined textbook-workbook approach. It
> cludes practical and easily understood discussion and examples
> the important statistics which teachers should master.

NOLL, VICTOR H., *Introduction to Educational Measurement*, Boste
Houghton Mifflin, 1957, 437 pp.
> This general measurement textbook presents two discussions
> statistics: Chapter 3 is an elementary discussion of informati
> essential to all teachers; Appendix A includes additional importa
> statistical computations which the more mathematically inclin
> teacher will find useful.

ndex

Index